Welcome to the wonderful worl
For a free short story and to list
chapter of all my other Regencies, p

CW01456620

https://romancenovelsbyglrobinson.com

Thank you!

G L Robinson

Héloïse Says No

A Regency Romance

By

GL Robinson

As always, in memory of my dear sister, Francine.

With thanks to my Beta Readers, who always tell me what they think.

And with special thanks to CS or his patient editing and technical help, and more especially, for his friendship.

Cover art: *Portrait of Miss Rosamond Croker*
by Sir Thomas Lawrence (British, 1769–1830)

ntents

Chapter One

London 1816

"Thank you for your flattering attention, my lord, but the answer is *no*."

So saying, Mrs. Héloise Ramsay curtseyed and left. Rory Compton, third Earl of Dexter and one of the most sought-after men in London, watched her go, anger narrowing his lips. Even so, he couldn't help admiring her shapely derrière as she crossed the room away from him. It was more than usually revealed because she had looped up the train of her ballgown onto her wrist and the shimmering overdress pulled at the silk beneath. To his mind, she was the most fascinating woman in London. Not as young as the girls in their first season, of course. He estimated she must be over twenty, but she was so very much more alluring than any of those damsels.

Lord Dexter was by then in his thirtieth year and even he would have agreed he'd been spoiled all his life. He had been born with the proverbial silver spoon in his mouth and with his good looks and charm had always been able to have his own way. His nanny had adored him, his tutors had been unable to reprimand him, he had been popular at school, both for his sporting ability and his open-handedness, and had sailed through Oxford with the minimum of effort and the maximum of charm.

His father was one of the Prince's cronies, both before and in the early days of his Regency, and followed him everywhere, with the result that as a boy, Rory saw him only rarely. He was therefore only dutifully fond of him and when he conveniently died during Rory's twenty-eighth year, he had not mourned his loss overlong. He had assumed the title and the fortune that went with it.

The only way this had materially affected his life was that his mother, whom he genuinely loved, had wanted to remove to a pleasant house overlooking one of the small parks for which London was well known. She had come to dislike the Dexter townhome with its large, cold rooms, filled with her husband's noisy and often intoxicated cronies. Rory had taken possession of it, as happy to be there as in his rather luxurious lodgings. Like everything else he owned, he let others run it. He occasionally met with his housekeeper, his agent, and his man of business, agreed with everything they said and left them, once again victims of his charm, to do whatever they saw fit.

He had been the darling of the *ton* ten seasons, though the mothers of hopeful maidens thrust into the marriage mart every year had long since given up on him. He was simply not interested in those young damsels, and indeed, never had been, even when younger himself.

He was well known to be rich enough, as the saying went, to buy an abbey, but preferred to spend his blunt on his stable. He was an expert rider, both in the hunt and with his racing curricle and pair, with which he regularly beat all-comers. Added to that, he was a good shot and a frequent visitor to Manton's shooting gallery on Davies Street. He was well known to be able to hit twelve wafers from a distance of fifteen yards in under the six minutes declared necessary for an expert. As a consequence, he was very rarely challenged to a duel, even when the wives of important gentlemen smiled a little too fondly at him.

He was popular in the Clubs, open handed at the card table, as good humored when he lost as when he won. He was a good dancer and never let his hostess down by playing cards all night and leaving partnerless females to sit in the corner all night.

But he seemed to have no interest at all in forming a permanent connection with any woman, or any connection at all with a young lady. For a month or two he would be seen with one or another lovely widow on his arm. Then she would appear with an expensive parure of jewelry and another would take her place. Mrs. Ramsay's refusal was the first check he had met with in his life.

She had appeared on the scene the year before, introduced by, of all people, Lady Pevensey, a very high flyer indeed. She had been presented as *the daughter of a friend of the family*, and such was her ladyship's unassailable position in the *ton* that no one had questioned who that friend might be, or where her daughter had come from.

It was all the more astonishing then, when it became apparent that Mrs. Ramsay was for temporary sale to anyone who would meet her price.

The first of these had been young Brownlow, just out of Cambridge and sowing some very wild oats indeed. For three months she graced his arm at the opera, at parties and anywhere the young and fashionable might go to see and be seen.

To be sure, she never entered the salons of Almack's, but whether that was because she chose not to go there or had been refused vouchers by the patronesses, no one ever knew. It was whispered behind more than one fan that it was unlikely even those ladies, so full of their own importance, would have dared refuse someone championed by Lady Pevensey. It was more probable Mrs. Ramsay herself had decided to avoid the venue. But she never said, and they dared not ask.

For the following three months Lionel Cartaret had been the lucky fellow to squire her. If Brownlow was young, Cartaret was, frankly, old. The *ton* was amazed when he took up with the lady. His wife had been dead these fifteen years and in that time he had never shown any interest in a possible replacement. Yet there he was, his somewhat bent back and bald head held perceptibly straighter as he accompanied the lovely lady everywhere. It had to be said, she treated him no differently from how she had treated Brownlow. She smiled kindly at him, spoke in an undertone, never embarrassed him by laughing too loud, playing roguishly with her fan or in any way acting otherwise than with perfect decorum.

Courtesan she might be, but it was very hard to dislike her. She was polite, self-effacing, and kind. She was as likely to spend half an hour talking to an ignored debutante in the corner as a wealthy peer. And even her few detractors had to admit she had a perfection of figure it was impossible to deny, and a face that held one's attention. Neither owed anything to artifice. She employed neither powder nor paint, nor, as far as one could tell, any corset, though she was very shapely, as Lord Dexter had once again irritably witnessed.

She had light brown curls unremarkable except for their abundance, and calm grey eyes fringed by very dark lashes. She was of average height, but her carriage made her appear taller, taller in fact, than the elderly Lord Cartaret. She dressed quietly but with elegance, danced gracefully, and when addressed spoke in pleasant tones, giving her interlocutor her whole attention without hesitation or coquetry.

If one examined her closely, as Lord Dexter had, one could often perceive the light of humor in her wide eyes, and her mouth had a tendency to curl up at the edges as if she were about to smile. Taken separately, nothing about her was truly remarkable, taken together, however, she really was quite irresistible. Lord Dexter had found it almost impossible, these last months, to take his eyes off her.

He was pipped at the post, however, when, at the end of three months with Cartaret, she appeared with Greville. Bryce Greville was a man of about his lordship's age. He had never married, nor, indeed seemed interested in women. He was a tall, thin, bookish fellow who, it was reported, studied the flora and fauna of his native Kent and was happier in a field than in the London salons. It was certainly true that for the period of her involvement with him, Mrs. Ramsay was often absent from the tonnish events of the season. But now, three months later, seeing her alone at the ball, Lord Dexter had thought it might be time to make his interest known.

Chapter Two

Paris 1792

"But, chéri, we must leave!" A very pretty lady dressed in a gown that was perhaps two years out of date but very becoming nonetheless, spoke urgently to her husband. "They've arrested the King and Queen and the violence against the nobility is growing worse every day. Why, Madame de Fortunay was pelted with stones in the street just yesterday. They are blamed for the poor harvest, the famine, everything!"

"But what has that to do with us, Claire?" answered her husband. "We aren't nobility. Not by any means!"

He was a tall, slightly stooped man in his early thirties. He had a pleasant face, and a charming smile. Without his glasses he could only see the world through a sort of haze, so he often looked a little lost.

"Of course we're not, but you know some people have taken exception to that article you wrote in the *Courrier Politique* about an ideal form of government. Bernard, you must know they think you support the monarchy."

"Well, I suppose I do, in a sense. A constitutional monarchy like they have in England. Why, everyone thought it was a good idea until the Jacobins started talking Republic. I spoke with

Robespierre myself and he was of the same opinion. He had nothing personal against the King. I can't imagine why they've arrested the royal family."

"I know nothing about politics but I do know that when Madame de Fortunay gets pelted in the street, intellectuals like you are not far behind. We must leave Paris—in fact we must leave France, especially now that I'm…." She unconsciously stroked her belly, where no bump could yet be discerned. "Let's go to England, if it's true they have the best form of *gouvernement*. Our son or daughter can grow up to be English (she pronounced it *Eengleesh*) and eat *ze rosbif.*" For it was the conviction of every French citizen that the English had a constant diet of roast beef. Johnny Bull was a popular cartoon figure representing the stout, beer swilling English.

"You're overreacting, my love," replied her husband with a laugh. "There's no need for us to go to England. I'm sure things will calm down here. You'll see. Though," he added as an afterthought, "a plate of *rosbif* would be very welcome. We've had nothing but stews of mostly vegetables for weeks. What's going on?"

"You know it's hard to get things these days," replied his wife. "I do the best I can!"

"Of course you do!" he cried, taking her by the waist and kissing her soundly. I'll eat boiled dandelions if you say I must."

In fact, for some months Claire had been quietly husbanding their resources. She was eking out the housekeeping by buying cheap cuts of meat requiring a great deal of cooking to make them edible, and bulking their diet up with vegetables. While she did not give her husband boiled dandelions, if she saw the young leaves of the plant emerging anywhere there was a little plot of green in the city, she quickly cut them and brought them home for salad. She had been bred in the country and knew the poor people ate them. They were held to be very healthy and known for their action on the kidneys, as the country name *pis-en-lit* (wet the bed) attested.

Apart from saving as much as she could from the household expenses, Claire had sewn her jewelry into the hem of her heavy travelling cloak. She had a few nice family pieces. When Claire Montignac had chosen Bernard Rambuteau, newly graduated from the university and with no financial expectations, her family had been at first surprised then resigned. They were well-to-do bourgeois wine merchants from Bordeaux and had hoped she would do better. But Bernard was a pleasant though serious and somewhat vague young man, and obviously adored her, as she adored him. He had plans to move to Paris and write for the newspapers, which, while it was not the most lucrative profession in the world, was socially acceptable. Besides, they had other daughters they needed to see safely settled.

So they had given their blessing, the couple had wed, moved to the capital and Bernard had done as he planned. His articles were inclined to be serious and over-learned, but a kindly editor had shown him how to tone down his rhetoric and even introduce a hint of whimsy. He had suggested the idea of researching customs in countries no one except dusty anthropologists had ever visited, and then writing up a sort of travelogue. These were completed with illustrations, often very fanciful, from an artist who had never been nearer any of the places he wrote about than Bernard had himself. At a time when the middle-class population of Europe had begun to think about lands outside their own shores, these columns had been very popular. For three years life for the Rambuteaus had been comfortable, if not luxurious.

Then in 1789 a mob, fueled by gossip, hunger, and general discontent, had stormed the Bastille prison, that symbol of repression, and life as they knew it had been changed forever. No one wanted travelogues any more. The newspapers were full of politics. Bernard was only interested in politics from the philosophical aspect and held no particular view. He had at first written articles about the Greeks and the Romans. No one took issue with them, other than they were rather dull. But then he made the mistake of writing about what constituted ideal government, of which he considered the constitutional monarchy and parliament of Britain a model.

At first this displeased only the monarchists who believed in French absolutism and wanted things left as they were. But when more and more radical elements began to emerge and decry the idea of monarchy altogether, his article was seen as anti-republican. In the end, it pleased neither faction.

Bernard, in his scholarly way, was unconcerned. After all, wasn't that the essence of compromise? A solution that pleased no one? But Claire was much more worried. She knew her husband was not very practical, but she was expecting a child and determined to raise it somewhere safe. She had at first thought about simply returning to Bordeaux. But Bordeaux was still France, and she had heard that violence was rife there too. So she had settled on England. She knew that a number of French nobles had taken refuge there, or in America, but that was much too far.

A week after their discussion, the Rambuteaus were sitting at lunch when a cobblestone came smashing through the window. Around it was wrapped a copy of Bernard's article. That settled it, thought Claire. They were leaving.

Chapter Three

Paris 1792

When Bernard and Claire had come to live in Paris, a married couple from the Montignac household in Bordeaux had come with them. Agnès had been Claire's nanny when she was not much more than a girl herself. She was a little, rounded person with apple cheeks and black eyes that sparkled when she was happy and glinted dangerously when she wasn't. When Claire no longer needed a nanny, Agnès stayed on as her maid.

Just about the time her young mistress had married, so had she. Her husband was Joseph Thomas, a tall, bull of a man hired in the household as a jack-of-all-trades. He could turn his hand to anything. Agnès barely came up to his armpit, but he was her slave and adored her. Agnès declared she was going to Paris with her mistress. And if Agnès was going, so was Joseph.

In fact, they were both excited to go to the capital, where they had never been. They were very happy as the only servants in the young couple's household. Agnès did the housekeeping, hiring an extra maid when she needed one, and was absolute mistress of the kitchen. She proved an excellent cook. Joseph carried in the wood for the fires, dealt with the stable where they kept their old horse Mimi and a gig, mended anything that needed it, and generally did whatever his wife told him.

Over these last weeks as Claire had made her preparations, she had involved Agnès and Joseph. She knew they couldn't manage without them.

"We have to leave," she said. "It's too dangerous for Monsieur here. The Jacobins think he supports the King."

"The Jacobins!" Joseph spat on the ground. "The devil take the lot of 'em."

"Hush, husband," said Agnès. "Someone may hear! Even the walls have ears."

"We're going to England," continued their mistress. "You do not have to come with us if you don't wish to. I don't expect it. You may stay here in the house or go back to Bordeaux, if you wish. The lease is paid till the end of the year and we'll give you as much money as we can. But we shall need your help getting out of Paris."

"You're not going anywhere without me, Madame," said Agnès stoutly. "I've not left you for more than a day or two since you was a baby. And I'll go bail my Joseph will say the same."

Joseph said simply, "If Agnès goes, I goes."

Tears came to Claire's eyes and she took them both by the hand. "Then we'll all go together," she said, "and God bless you!"

"Joseph," she said, giving him a roll of money just a couple of days later, "trade in the gig for a cart. Nothing too fine. A strong farmer's vehicle, if you can, in reasonable condition. I'm afraid we must trade in poor old Mimi too, for a good horse to pull it and us. You may need extra money, especially for the horse. Use up these *Assignats* first. People don't trust that paper money, for all that it's new and supposed to be better. I'm sure the coins will be more use to us later on, away from the capital. And we'll need as many old sacks as you can get. Perhaps twenty. Then I want you to fill six or seven of the sacks with horse manure."

He thought he had misheard. "Horse shi... manure, Madame?"

"Yes. You don't mind shoveling it up from the streets, do you?"

Like all big cities, Paris had almost as many horses as people. Picking up the manure was a common occupation.

"No, Madame, I've shoveled enough of it in my time, the good Lord knows!"

"And I want you to bury the candlesticks and little wine cups from the salon and all the silver cutlery in one of the bags of manure."

"Bury the silver in shi...? I beg your pardon, Madame," said Joseph, his eyes round.

"Yes, we can sell it when we get to England. French money won't be any good for us there."

This meant that on the day the cobblestone came through the window, a new horse was waiting in the yard behind the house. He was munching peaceably on a nosebag of fodder while behind him stood a cart filled with piles of empty potato sacks and half a dozen more very malodorous ones. One of them was significantly heavier than its neighbors.

Luckily the cobblestone throwing mob had not stormed the house, content to continue up the street smashing other windows. The arrest of the royal family and the news that the King and Queen were to stand trial had resulted in drunken jubilation and the lawless behavior typical of mobs. As Bernard remarked, anyone who has studied history knows no matter how justified the original reason for civil unrest, it inevitably ends up led by thugs who enjoy destruction for its own sake. Now they could hear snatches of a new song that had been making an appearance in the streets of the capital these last few months. Apparently it had first been heard in the southern town of Marseille. They didn't know it, but it would become the national anthem of France. *Allons enfants de la patrie*....

"Chéri," said Claire calmly. "You know we have to leave. The mob has identified you as the writer of that article. They'll be back. Go upstairs, put on your warmest suit and cloak, and your stoutest boots. Bring any cash you have, your watch and fob but nothing else."

"But... my books...."

"No, I'm sorry, no books."

"But...."

"We take nothing but what we can carry. Books are too heavy. Please, chéri, you know I'm right."

Bernard looked at her solemnly and nodded. "Of course you're right. You always are!"

He went upstairs and did as he was bid. Before returning to his wife, he put his head into the small room he had used as his office and library. He inhaled deeply, savoring one last time the scent of old leather and paper he found so delicious, so comforting. As he turned to leave, he noticed the slim volume of Rousseau's *La Nouvelle Héloïse* (*The New Héloise*) on the table. He had read it aloud to his wife when they were first married. They had both loved it.

In a series of letters, Rousseau tells the story of a high-bred young woman forced to give up the impoverished man she loves. She nonetheless lives a contented life as wife to the man her parents chose for her. When her first love comes back into the picture as tutor to her children, they are able to live in harmony all together. The nobly expressed sentiments and the importance of the domestic scene where Héloise holds sway especially appealed to Claire. On impulse, Bernard picked it up and put it in the capacious pocket of his cloak.

Under an hour later, Claire and Bernard were lying in the back of the cart, on top of folded coverlets from their beds and covered with the old sacks. Joseph had carefully loaded the dung-filled sacks around them. Agnès had given her pregnant mistress a sachet of lavender to hold under her nose, and as the cart began to make its ponderous and jerky way over the cobbles, Claire thanked God for it. Bile rose in her throat and it was all she could do not to vomit. She clung to her husband's hand and tried to think of the pine forests of her childhood, and the smell of the sea beyond the sand dunes.

Joseph drove the horse with Agnès sitting next to him. They had both done the same as Monsieur and Madame and were wearing their heaviest clothing and warmest cloaks, though it was late April and the freezing days of winter were over. The worst problem would be the rain. It always rained in northern France in April.

They arrived without incident at the Barrière de la Chapelle, one of the tax gates in the north of the city. The wall through which it gave access had been completed within the last twenty years. It was not for defense, as the old walls had been, but to collect taxes on farm goods entering Paris.

This was the moment Claire had feared. Passing through these barrières in anything more luxurious than a farm cart would have surely marked them as a member of the privileged class and they could well have been turned back. Look what had happened to the King and Queen! She had decided they would be safer hidden as they were, in a cart ostensibly returning to a farm outside the city.

She need not have worried. Joseph was up to the task.

"Holà citizens!" he called to the waiting guards. "Paid me tax on the way in this mornin'. Nothing but empty sacks and horse-shit here!"

"What d'you mean?" asked one of them. He left his post and approached the cart. "God in heaven, what's that stink?"

"Like I said, empty sacks and horse-shit," said Joseph cheerfully. "We brings in the potatoes and we fills as many sacks as we can with horse-shit to take back to grow more. We got the best spuds in the country. Ask anyone!"

"Don't you got no horse-shit out there in the country?" asked the guard, standing way back from the odiferous cart.

"Sure we do, but not as much as you got in the city—in more ways than one." Joseph roared at his own joke and slapped his knee.

"You watch your mouth, peasant," said the guard, nevertheless motioning them to pass.

"Just my little joke, yer honor. Good day to you, citizen!" said Joseph. He clicked up the horse and they ambled through the gate.

Chapter Four

Northern France 1792

Hidden under the sacks in the bottom of the cart, Claire and Bernard held their breaths until they thought the city wall must be well behind them. Then, about thirty minutes later, they felt the cart drawing to a halt and their hearts were again in their mouths until the voice of Agnès came from above them.

"Monsieur! Madame!" she said, "You can come out now. There's no one around. Nothing but fields. Joseph and me, we'll climb in the back. You sit up front."

With enormous relief, Claire and Bernard sat up and looked at each other.

"Well," said Bernard. "That's a story to tell our little one." He patted his wife's stomach.

Claire was pale, but she smiled. "Yes indeed," she said, "but I must…."

Unable to say another word, she scrambled down from the cart and ran to the ditch on the side of the road. There, with Agnès beside her, she retched and retched, until, exhausted, she sank to the ground.

"The cognac, Joseph, quick!" said Agnès. From a capacious bag they had not noticed until that point, Joseph produced a bottle and a small cup.

"I thought it best to bring a little something, just in case," explained Agnès, and poured out about a thimbleful, which she urged on Claire.

"Drink this, Madame," she said. "It'll do you good."

And although it burned all the way down and made her choke a little, Claire had to admit a few moments later, she did feel somewhat better. With her husband's help, she climbed up onto the front of the cart. Then Bernard took the reins, and with Agnès and Joseph sitting up with their backs against the footboard, they clip-clopped down the road.

The journey to Calais, where they would find a boat to sail them across the channel, would take three days. Bernard, the scholar, knew the map of his homeland as well as his own name and was able to lead them unerringly north.

The first night, darkness fell when they were nowhere near any sort of town, so they sought shelter in a farmhouse. Whether or not the farmer and his wife believed their story about being on their way to visit relatives, they did believe the offer of several bags of good horse manure. They permitted the group to bed down in the hayloft, showed them where the pump and the privy were, and left them to it.

Joseph had beguiled the afternoon and evening journey by extracting the silver from the odiferous sack where he had hidden it, and cleaning it on an empty one. As the light failed, he claimed it had never looked so good. It certainly glinted in the moonlight. He then rolled it up in several pieces of cut-up sacking and tied it in a bundle, which he took with him when they left the cart.

The horse was fed and watered, and Monsieur and Madame were prepared to go to sleep hungry when Agnès revealed more contents of the bag she had brought 'Just In Case'. There was bread and sausage and an apple each. Nothing had ever tasted better, particularly when washed down with a bottle of just-in-case wine and cold water from the pump.

The two couples took the coverlets from the cart, lay them on piles of hay and settled down at a discreet distance from each other. Then, still feeling the bumping of the cart and with the smell of manure still in their noses from the coverlets, all four fell asleep, their dreams populated by guards, potato sacks, shiny candelabra and cobblestones crashing through windows. Joseph slept clutching the sack of silver.

They were woken by the crowing of the cock at first light and arose slowly, feeling twinges of aches and pains from the previous day's bumpy ride. The morning was chilly, and they were glad of their heavy cloaks. As they led the horse and cart into the yard, the farmer's wife must have heard them. After the conventional greeting of whether they had slept well, she invited them into the kitchen for a bowl of soup.

As in all country kitchens, a large pot stood on the side of the fire and into it went scraps of everything left over. Sometimes it would be little more than watery cut-up vegetables, but sometimes, and this was one of them, it would be flavored with a ham bone. This unexpected act of kindness cheered them almost more than the hot soup itself. With salutations of good luck on either side, they left in a cheerful and encouraged frame of mind.

This did not last. It turned into miserable day, raining on and off, so that even covering themselves tightly with their cloaks, they were drenched. Bernard was particularly afflicted. From childhood he had suffered from a weak chest and his skinny frame easily caught cold. Claire made him lie in the cart, covered with all the sacks and the coverlets, but still he shivered.

"We must find an inn for tonight," she announced, "no matter what it costs. Monsieur must have a warm, dry bed. And we must dry our clothes. We cannot arrive in England all suffering from the *grippe.*"

The rain eased as night fell and they at last straggled into a small town that boasted not one, but two, inns. Choosing the better looking of the two, Claire and Agnès boldly entered and requested two rooms for the night and somewhere to dry their clothes.

The innkeeper looked them over and laughed, "And what might two persons like you be doing on the road in this weather and unaccompanied?" he sniffed, "And smelling of the farmyard, besides!"

"We are not unaccompanied," replied Claire with hauteur. "Our husbands are waiting outside."

"Fine men they must be, sending their women in here. Be off with you. In any case, we have no room!"

At the smaller inn, the two men tried their luck. Bernard was by now looking feverish. Two spots of color were high on his cheeks and his eyes looked unnaturally bright. The innkeeper was more polite, and apologized for having no room.

"It's market day tomorrow, you see," he explained. "People come in for the night. Now if you'd come yesterday...."

Bernard reached for his handkerchief in his pocket and in so doing, pulled out the slim volume of Rousseau's *The New Héloise.*

It fell to the floor. Seeing it, the landlord exclaimed, *"The New Héloise*! My God, that's my wife's favorite book! She had a lot more schooling than me!" he added proudly. "She was quite the bookworm before we were married! If we'd had a daughter, we would've called her Héloise." He shouted into the back room, "Come and look at this, Hélène! Monsieur has a copy of your favorite book!"

The landlady bustled in, drying her hands on her apron. She picked up the book. "My goodness!" She looked dreamily into the distance as if remembering a happy past. "My godmother was married to a well-to-do merchant and gave me this book as a gift when I turned sixteen. How many times I read it when I was a girl. Your copy is in much better condition than mine. I swear I almost wore out the pages!"

Then she noticed Bernard's feverish condition. "But why are you keeping this poor man standing here like this, Jean? He's soaking wet. Anyone can see he's poorly and needs a hot toddy and a bed."

"But we don't have a spare…."

"Nonsense! He can go in that back room. Old Duboeuf hasn't turned up yet, and if he does he can share with our lad."

"But we are four, Madame," said Bernard with difficulty. His chest was feeling as if iron bars were enclosing it. He gasped. "My wife and our two servants, Joseph here and his wife. And a horse and cart."

"Oh, the bed in that back room is large enough for you and your wife and your people can sleep in a corner of the kitchen, if they're willing. It's warm and dry and I've got a mattress somewhere. My Emile will take care of the horse. Don't you worry!"

"Emile, Madame?" Bernard smiled in spite of the hammers in his head that had joined forces with the iron bands in his chest. "Don't tell me you were able to read Rousseau's book by that name too?

"No. I wanted to, but it was forbidden, as you know. I always remembered the name and when I had my boy that's what I called him."

An hour later, Bernard was in a warm bed with shawl around his shoulders and a hot brick at his feet. Agnès and Joseph were in the kitchen helping the landlady get dinner ready for the many hungry customers crowding the inn, and next to the huge fireplace Claire was hanging up as much of the wet clothing as they could all remove.

She took a hot concoction of lemons, sugar and Agnès's brandy up to her husband and sat with him reading from the book that had saved them until he fell asleep. Later on she went downstairs and had a bowl of soup in the dining room. It was full of farmers who had arrived for the market the next day, and the room smelled of a combination of farmyard boots and mutton stew. It was noisy and cheerful, and if she hadn't been so worried about her husband, she would have enjoyed it.

Chapter Five

Northern France 1792

Overnight, Bernard's condition worsened. He ran a high fever and threw off all the bedcovers, alternating with periods of shivering when his wife couldn't pile enough on him. Early the next morning she found the landlady and begged to send for a doctor.

"Oh, you don't need a doctor," she said. "I'll get old Madeleine. She'll cup him and give him one of her tisanes. He'll be right as a trivet. You'll see."

Claire was more than skeptical when old Madeleine arrived. She was stooped and gnarled, like a tree standing in constant wind. Her black gown and cloak were rusty with age, but her eyes were bright and she seemed to know what she was doing. She had Bernard lie on his front, and she rubbed his back gently with an oil smelling of a plant Claire thought she should recognize.

"*Hysope*," murmured the old lady. "I'll give him a tisane of it in a minute. I've been making it for years. It does the trick with an inflammation of the lungs."

Out of a capacious sack-like bag, not unlike the one Agnès carried, she took a number of small, wide glasses. She lit a candle and one by one, heated the inside of the glasses and plopped them on Bernard's back. His wife saw the skin under the glass puff up and turn red. Madeleine left them there for a few minutes, then popped them off. There was a distinct sucking sound as each glass came clear and there were round marks all over Bernard's back.

"Draws out the humors," said Madeleine. "There's some as make little cuts in the center of each, but I don't hold with it. I've seen too many of the cuts go bad."

She gently massaged more of the oil over Bernard's back, pulled down his shirt and told him to turn over. He should try to sit up, she said, not lie down flat. She went downstairs and came back with a cup of a pale liquid.

"Now, you have him drink this and then he'll sleep," she said. "You should get some rest too, young lady. You look done in and it's not good for the baby. Oh yes," she said, as Claire's eyes widened in surprise. Her stomach was still perfectly flat. "I know there's a baby in there. I can see the signs."

Claire gladly gave the old lady one of their jealously horded coins. She bit it with her discolored teeth and cackled. "He'll be all right. But he'll never be strong, you know. I've seen a lot of 'em like him. But give him some more of the tisane when he wakes up. He'll be able to get up by tomorrow."

Claire lay down next to her drowsy husband holding his hand. Just for a minute, she thought, then she'd get up and make sure their clothes were drying evenly and give them a good brushing. At least the rain would have got rid of most of the smell of manure! Just for a minute. But in spite of herself, her eyes closed and soon she was fast asleep, curled next to her husband.

It was well into the afternoon before Claire awoke, and she was relieved to see Bernard sound asleep, his breathing even. His

26

color was much better. She sat up, and her stirring made him open his eyes. He smiled at her, then closed them again. She tidied her brown curls and crept from the room. Downstairs the inn was quiet, the shoppers from the market and farmers who had flooded in for a noon-time meal now gone. But the air was still redolent of the food they had served.

She sniffed and felt a pang of hunger. She slipped into the kitchen and saw Agnès and Joseph sitting at the scrubbed deal table with their host and hostess, a bottle of wine open between them. When they saw her, they all leaped to their feet and Agnès ran over.

"Madame! How is Monsieur? I peeped in earlier but you were both in a fine sleep. God be praised! Go into the dining room. I'll bring you something to eat directly."

"I don't like to put you to any bother. A cup of tea and a piece of bread and cheese would…," she began.

"Nonsense!" replied the landlady. "You have had nothing all day. And we are finished much earlier than usual. Dear Agnès and Joseph have been such a help!"

Claire noticed they were using first names and smiled. She knew Agnès would work as long as there was work to be done, and Joseph was ready for anything. She would have liked to sit in the kitchen with them, but she knew it would make them all uncomfortable, so she went into the dining room. The tables had all been cleared and without the cheerful chatter of the night before, it looked forlorn. But the remains of a fire glowed gently in the grate, and she chose a table close to it.

In a few minutes Agnès came in with a tray carrying a plate of what looked like stew, a hunk of bread and a glass of red wine.

"Elegant it isn't, Madame," she said. "I wouldn't serve you like this at home but...."

"It smells delicious, Agnès. And we must get used to things being different now. In fact, they will surely never go back to how they used to be. All I pray is that we shall be safe and make a new life in England for our little one." She smiled a little sadly at her faithful helper.

"Don't you worry. Joseph and I will look after you and Monsieur."

"And we shall look after you. We will look after each other, just as they are saying in the streets of Paris: liberty, equality, fraternity."

They looked at each other, not as mistress and servant, but as two women a little afraid of what lay ahead, but determined to make the best of it.

The following morning Bernard was, as Madeleine had predicted, very much better. He had woken and eaten a plate of soup the night before and overnight his breathing remained unlabored. Leaning on Joseph's arm, he was able to get down the stairs. When he got to the bottom he reached into his pocket and took out the copy of *The New Héloise*.

"Madame," he said to the landlady. "Please take this copy of the book we both love. Give me your old one. It will be a pleasure for me to read it and think of you."

He had to press her to take it, but in the end she did, and the exchange was made. Claire tried to pay for their two nights' lodging, but this was refused.

"Nay, Madame," said the landlady. "I'm well paid enough with this new book, besides the work Agnès and Joseph done for us.

And Joseph's stories about Paris, well, they gave us all a good laugh. That's worth more these days than all those *Assignats*. Useless bits of paper they try to tell us is money! Bah!"

Their cloaks and the coverlets had all been dried and brushed, and in spite of his protests, Claire insisted on wrapping her husband up. She sat with him in the back of the cart and with fond farewells and invitations to return, they set out on the last leg of the trip to Calais.

"Do you think we'll ever come back?" she said to Bernard as they clip-clopped their way down the road.

"I don't know," he replied with a sad smile. "Our son or daughter will be English. So we must become English too. We won't forget France, but in time it will mean less and less, I think."

"At least our last memory of the people will be good," said Claire, trying not to think about leaving everything and everyone she had ever known. "The farmer's wife our first night and the landlord and lady of the inn were all kind to us. They are the real France, not those screaming mobs in Paris."

And on that last day in their homeland, the sun shone. It was a weak spring sun, but it cheered their hearts and as they turned their faces up to it, it seemed to promise them a better future.

Chapter Six

Calais 1792

But they almost lost faith in the promise of a better future during the trip from Calais to Dover. It was appalling. If they had known what was in store, they probably would have given up there and then.

Bernard had decided there would be less risk of running into officials who might ask awkward questions if they avoided the town of Calais itself. It was well known that over the years there had been plans to attack Britain from this closest point, and if they were seen trying to get across the Channel, Bernard had no confidence that the authorities would not consider them English sympathizers and try to stop them.

Towards the end of the afternoon they therefore found themselves riding up the coast towards Calais, looking out over the wide beaches for any sign of a sailboat that might take them. Having grown up in Bordeaux which lies on an estuary leading to the Atlantic Ocean, they all knew that apart from a sea-worthy vessel, the other vital factors in sea travel were the wind and the tide.

Looking at the way the wind ruffled the rather sparse vegetation, Joseph held his nose into it and declared it would be a hard crossing. The wind was onshore and it looked like the tide was on the turn. They wondered if they should stop in France another night, but decided to risk it. There was no guarantee it would be better tomorrow.

The sun was beginning to go down by the time they came into the fishing village of Sangatte and saw a man sitting on an upturned barrel next to a fishing boat, smoking a pipe and looking at the tide. Joseph immediately engaged him in a conversation that involved a good deal of head-scratching, looking at the cart and its occupants, gazing up into the sky and waving the pipe around.

"He'll do it," said Joseph, coming back finally, "for the price of the horse and cart and 250 *livres*. "But he says we better go quick. As I thought, the tide is on the change."

"Done," said Claire, quickly. "I can give him the *Assignats* I have left. It might not be 250 *livres* but it's enough. They'll be no good to us in England anyway. Tell him he gets the horse and cart now and the money when we get there. I'll show him the roll of money, but I won't give it to him until my feet are on the beach in England."

Bernard looked at her and laughed. "My gently-reared wife!" he said. "I didn't know you could drive such a hard bargain!"

"I'm learning all sorts of things," she said gaily, though her heart was thumping in her chest. Now it was real—they were actually leaving.

The sailor called to a knot of men in a language none of the travelers could understand, but the result was that two detached themselves from the group and came over. One took the horse's bridle and the other, helped by Joseph who reluctantly set the sack of silver by Monsieur's feet, dragged the boat down to the water.

Agnès reached into her capacious bag. She had shopped at the market the day before and had kept them provisioned during the long day's ride. She took out an apple, which she fed to the horse. She patted it on the nose and for a moment watched it and the cart being led away. Then she turned, and she and Claire helped Bernard down to the boat, still wrapped in the coverlets.

The tide was just at the turn and the sea was dreadfully choppy. The wind was blowing almost directly in their faces, so they had to tack endlessly. This made for very slow, uncomfortable progress. It was also wet and cold. Waves splashed over the gunwales every time they went about, and the bottom of the boat soon began to fill with water. There was sort of canvas cover over a makeshift platform in the bow, and Claire forced Bernard to stay in there. He tried to give the place to her, or to make her lie down with him, but she was so seasick she could do nothing but retch over the side. Joseph looked distinctly queasy and was far from his usual cheerful self. The only one who seemed unaffected was Agnès. She tried to help Claire by giving her tiny sips of the brandy she still had in her bag, but she could keep nothing down. Finally, from sheer exhaustion, Claire lay beside her husband and slept fitfully.

The two sailors cocked an eye at the brandy bottle but Agnès put it firmly away, saying, "I'll give you a nip when we get there and not before."

She spent the rest of the trip helping the captain's mate bail water from the bottom of the boat. Apart from hauling on the sails every time they went about, that seemed to be his main job. She got quite friendly with him, or as much as she could be with a man of whose utterances she understood about one word in ten. She found out later from Monsieur that he was probably speaking Breton, a language quite unlike French. This was chiefly spoken in Brittany, but Breton seamen were known to go anywhere along the coast they could get work.

The crossing, which was under thirty miles, could be done in as little as three hours. It took them nine. As the dawn broke, they got their first glimpse of the famous white cliffs of Dover, off to the right in the distance. However, the cliffs all but disappeared as they got closer into shore. When at last the mariners dropped the sails and hauled the boat onto the beach, the land lay flat before them. That was deemed a very good thing by at least two of the travelers. The prospect of dragging themselves up those towering cliffs paths after that dreadful crossing was daunting. They were all cold, wet and exhausted. They told themselves nothing would ever induce them to make that trip again. France was truly gone forever.

Agnès once again proved her worth by persuading the sailors to carry Claire onto the strand. Then, when Bernard tried to stand, it was clear he would have to be all but carried too. Joseph wanted to help but was so queasy and unstable it was as much as he could do to keep himself up straight. At length they were all installed on the pebbly beach beyond the high tide mark. Claire found the roll of *Assignats* and handed it to the sailors. Agnès gave them the rest of the bottle of brandy, which appeared to cheer them more than the money. To the amazement of the passengers, who nothing could have induced to step a foot back in the boat, they got right back on board and prepared to leave.

"Got us a nice little run back," said the captain. "Wind'll be aft all the way across. We'll do it in a wink."

The mate said something incomprehensible and saluted Agnès. Then he and the captain pushed the vessel back into the waves, hauled up the sails and opened them wide on both sides. Sure enough, in a matter of minutes, it seemed, they had disappeared.

Chapter Seven

England 1792

They all began to feel better the minute their feet were on dry land, even if the dry land was a beach of pebbles unlike any they had ever seen. Then from her inexhaustible bag Agnès produced some bread and cheese and a small dark bottle. She gave them all a sip. Claire grimaced, but Joseph and Bernard welcomed it.

"Ah! Calvados," said Bernard, with a wheeze in his voice. "Made from the apples of Normandy. What a treat!" He smiled at Agnès and took the piece of the rather dry bread she held out to him, along with a piece of a soft cheese. "And Camembert! Agnès, you are a marvel!"

Claire couldn't face the cheese, but the bread and the nip of Calvados helped settle her stomach. Then she stood up and looked behind them.

They seemed to be at the straggling end of a small town or village nestled between two hills. Her heart sank. To get to London, they would have to get over those hills. They would need a horse and carriage or cart of some type. And how many days travel would it be? Bernard was simply too weak for a long trip at the moment, and she wasn't sure she could face it herself.

She made a decision. "Joseph, please get the set of silver teaspoons out of the sack, and let's go find an inn where we can rest up. Agnès, you will stay with Monsieur, won't you?"

"Of course, Madame, but don't be surprised if we're both as drunk as lords by the time you return!"

Joseph, who had found his land legs, helped her to her feet, gave her the silver teaspoons and slung the sack with the rest of the silver over his shoulder. Over their protests that it was too heavy to carry he said, "Me and this silver, we're not parted till we gets where we're going."

There was no changing his mind, so he and Claire set off in the direction of the few houses they could see off to the left.

A short way along the straggle of poor-looking dwellings there was an inn. The exterior was patched, the paintwork peeling and the mullioned window that gave onto the road was so dirty they could see nothing through it. They looked at each other doubtfully, but Claire shrugged. What choice did they have?

They entered together to see a slatternly looking woman pushing a dirty cloth over a table in the one room that seemed to constitute most of the ground floor of the establishment. Claire began, knowing her English was far from perfect.

"Madame," she said, "We are arrive from France in boat. We seek chamber. We are four persons. My 'usband, 'e goes not good."

"'E looks all right to me," said the woman, looking Joseph up and down.

"No eez not my 'usband. Eez my...."

38

"Well, if you think you're a-comin' 'ere with a bloke wot's not yer 'usband, yer can push off again," said the woman, and continued wiping the dirty cloth around the tables.

Claire did not at once understand what she had said, but after running the words through in her mind, responded, "Mais non, Madame. My 'usband 'e eez on zee, 'ow you say, stones." She gestured back the way they had come. "'E not walk so far. 'E need carriage."

"Carriage? You think we've got a carriage? "'Orse and cart is what we got, if you can pay." She rubbed her thumb and first finger together in the universal sign for money.

Claire produced a silver teaspoon from her pocket. The landlady took it and bit it.

"Real silver that is," she declared. "Ow many you got?"

Claire made a show of searching around in her pocket and finally took out a second spoon. "Two spoon for 'orse and...?" she wrinkled her brow trying to think what the woman had said.

"Cart," supplied the landlady. "Two spoons for the 'orse and cart to fetch yer 'usband?"

"And two chamber for night." Claire lifted her chin. "Is good spoons."

The landlady looked at her, then at the spoons. They had no one staying in the inn, in fact they rarely had anyone these days. The troubles in France had put an end to most of the travelers who occasionally spent the night there before going on to Dover.

"All right. That'll do," she said. Then with a jerk of her chin, "Come along wi' me."

She led them out the back of the building, through a dirty scullery where a pile of pots stood on a table, a pair of marmalade color cats licking them.

"Get off, yer dirty buggers!" she said, ineffectually swinging her apron at them.

They lifted their heads but otherwise paid no attention. Joseph looked at Claire and curled his lip.

In a lean-to on the back there was a mangy-looking horse and an ancient cart. It hardly looked as if it would make it half a mile down the road before falling to pieces, but beggars couldn't be choosers. Claire gave the second spoon to the landlady, Joseph helped her up onto the wooden plank seat and then climbed up himself. He clicked to the horse and reluctantly the animal moved forward. The vehicle was in far worse condition than the one they had traded with the sailors, but creaking and rattling, it carried them back to the beach where Bernard and Agnès were waiting.

The pair were laughing as they drew up.

"Madame!" cried Agnès. "Monsieur is teaching me English. It's a barbarous language, for sure. Listen, Joseph. I'll speak to you in English. *Gud merning, Joseph. 'Ow are you t'day?* Now you have to say, *Verray will, zank you.*"

"I ain't saying no such thing," responded Joseph. "And you won't be so full of joy when you see the place we're going to be staying in. I lay my oath the beds is full of fleas and damp besides."

"As bad as that?" said Bernard, looking at his wife.

"Probably, but we'll make it work. We can wash the sheets. It's going to be a nice day, I think.

40

"If I can get some mint or some cloves to put on the mattresses, the fleas don't like that," said Agnès. "Anyway, we'll manage. It will be *verray will, zank you!*"

Bernard and Claire laughed and Joseph shook his head fondly.

When they arrived back at the inn, they noticed a faded and cracked board above the door bearing the legend: *The Traveller's Rest. Prop. Josiah Parrish*.

"Look at that," said Claire. She translated the sign for Agnès and Joseph. "It's a good omen! But I wonder who Josiah Parrish might be. We saw no one but a woman, and to judge from the condition of the place, she's alone."

Chapter Eight

Hastings 1792

They were to find later that Josiah Parrish did exist. He was at that moment sleeping off a night of heavy drinking and wouldn't put in an appearance until much later in the day. By that time, ignoring the complaints from the landlady who she couldn't understand anyway, Agnes had stripped the linen off the beds in the two largest bedchambers and had boiled it all in pots of water in the hovel of a kitchen.

When she went to hang the sheets and pillow slips outside, she found clumps of mint growing behind the privy. Holding her nose, she picked a large bunch. She used the hot water from the washing to mop the kitchen floor, disturbing spiders, and nests from which the mice had fled in terror, before throwing it, absolutely black, down the stinking hole in the grim little hut of the privy.

Declaring that Monsieur and Madame were not going to use anything in the state it was in, she set Joseph to shovel the ashes from the cold hearth in the saloon down there as well. Then she had him bring the mattresses from their bedchambers down to air in the sun on top of the bushes behind the inn, and to sprinkle them liberally with mashed mint leaves. Finally, they both went back and forth to the pump, filling pails of water for the cleaning of the pots, pans, and dishes.

In spite of Agnès' protestations, Claire tucked her skirts up into her waistband and donned a dirty apron to begin this momentous task. Bernard protested at being made to sit still while all this activity was going on, so Agnès set him on a chair next to the bedsteads to rub the frames and mattress strapping with handfuls of mint leaves. The scent filled his nose and in fact improved his breathing. He approached it with a seriousness of purpose that made his wife laugh when she went to see what he was doing.

She kissed the top of his head. *Verray will, zank you*, she said. He pulled her onto his knee and hugged her.

"I'm glad we left France," he said. "Thank you for making me do it. Sitting here, my hands green with mint and the smell of it in my nose, knowing you and the little one are safe," he caressed her still flat stomach, "I can't think of anything better. Except a cup of coffee?" He looked at her hopefully.

"Sorry, I haven't seen any in that place that passes for a kitchen. But it's nearly cleaned up down there and Agnès is looking for something to call lunch. I keep thinking she'll just go on producing things from that bag of hers!" She kissed him again and went downstairs.

The landlady had given up complaining and even joined in, sweeping the floor with a broom that became less and less effective as it lost its straws. The two marmalade cats watched suspiciously from the kitchen door and only dared creep back in when she left to go outside, carrying a bowl. She reappeared a few minutes later with 6 eggs.

"Hen house," she said shortly and pointed.

It turned out that the inn had not only a hen house but an apple orchard off to one side.

As Claire had predicted, it had turned into a nice day. The sun shone warmly from a blue sky. Joseph was directed to carry one of the tables and five chairs outside under the apple trees. Agnès made a scramble with the eggs, divided it between five now clean plates and put them on the table, together with the rest of the bread and cheese from her bag. The landlady disappeared again and came up from a cellar that no one knew existed, bearing a foaming jug.

"Cider," she said. "From the apples." She pointed to the branches above their heads.

They enjoyed their lunch more than they would have thought possible when they had arrived. They toasted their arrival in England and the meeting of another friend, in the unlikely person of the landlady. As they sat together, she came out of her shell and told them her name was Ivy. Ivy Parrish.

Though nothing was said, she seemed to absorb the distinction between Bernard and Claire and Agnès and Joseph, calling the former *M'sure* and *M'dame* and the latter by their first names. She disclosed to Bernard, whose English was much better than his wife's and whose smile was hard to resist, that she and her husband used to run a fairly thriving business, between the locals who came for the home-brew and chance visitors stopping on their way to or from Dover. They made their own cider and beer, the remains of which were in the cellar. They were helped out by their two youngsters: a son and a daughter.

Then three years before, their son had died in a fishing accident. He had gone out to help a friend and they'd been caught in a sudden squall. Her husband had taken it very hard.

Nowadays he would install himself in the corner of the downstairs room and his glass would be full from before the first customer arrived until after the last one left. Then he'd take the whole morning to sleep it off. They had a daughter who used to help out, but she had married the year before and had moved to London where her husband's family lived.

"She weren't wantin' to go, but 'er 'usband insisted and I tole 'er she oughta go where she could 'ave a good life. I can manage on me own. Got to. 'E ain't much 'elp."

At that point a shuffling step could be heard and a grumbling voice called out, "Where are yer? Wot's goin' on?" and the landlord appeared.

His grizzled chin showed several days growth of beard and his clothing was stained and filthy. He was under average height but had extra girth to make up for it. His shirt and waistcoat must have been made for him when he was a smaller man, for they no longer met across his pale hairy stomach. His belly hung slackly over his britches. He scratched at it as he came towards them and his strong odor met their noses almost before he was close enough to take in the details of the al fresco lunch party.

"'Oo are you lot, then?" he asked belligerently. Bernard stood and held out his hand, which the other man ignored. "Bernard Rambuteau," he said. "And this is my wife Claire and our...," he hesitated, "our friends Agnès and Joseph Thomas."

"A load of Frenchies?" he turned to his wife. "Wot they doin' 'ere?"

"Eatin' their dinner like Christians, and cooked it too, not to mention cleanin' the kitchen, that's what," retorted Ivy. "And their money's as good as anyone's."

46

She failed to mention the silver spoons and no one enlightened him.

"Fine thing, I comes down an' me own wife's eatin' outside like a gypsy wiv a bunch of foreigners. And nothin' fer me, I spose?"

"Yer always wantin' ter eat but don't do nothin' to put food on the table," she complained, but then relented. "There's a lump o' bread an' a bite o' their cheese. It's a bit odd, like, but not bad."

"Bah!" her husband stumbled off to the hedge that ran the length of the orchard, and relieved himself copiously into it. Then he came back, grabbed the piece of bread and the remains of the cheese, took what was left of the cider and staggered back indoors.

As his wife had said, he spent the rest of the day in the corner of the main room, gazing morosely into his glass and descending to the cellar to top up the jug. The others washed up the lunch plates and finished cleaning the kitchen. While Agnès explored the cellar, Claire mopped the bedroom floors, glad to be able to do it without her faithful helper seeing. She would have scolded and taken the mop from her hands, saying that was not a fit job for Madame. But as Claire saw it, all jobs were now fit for Madame.

Unaware of her intransigence, Agnès searched around the cellar, disturbing spiders and mice living peacefully in corners for years. She determined that the cats who had been licking the pots in the kitchen needed more gainful employment. She'd shut them in the cellar for a couple of nights. Apart from a row of wooden casks, most of which appeared to be empty, she found a quantity of shriveled root vegetables and a desiccated flitch of bacon. Both showed signs of mice dining, but she thought that with a good scrub and boiling in several changes of water, they wouldn't do anyone any harm.

She brought these treasures upstairs and before long the kitchen was redolent of soup simmering at the edge of the fire. The landlord stirred himself from his corner and came in, sniffing like an old dog. Joseph brought in the mattresses and put them back on the mint-covered bedframes. They lay down to rest under their own coverlets, stained here and there from their adventures in the haybarn and the cart and stiff from salt water. But whatever the combination was, it seemed to deter the fleas. They slept soundly for a couple of hours, dust motes dancing above them and the warm sun attempting to shine through the dirty mullioned windows.

"Got to clean those windows," was Agnès's last thought before she fell asleep next to her husband.

Chapter Nine

London 1816

Gradually, no one knew how, since the gentlemen concerned had been doggedly closed-lipped, it had become common knowledge in the clubs that Mrs. Ramsay demanded just three things of her protectors. First, that their "friendship" would be of a period of no more than three months not extendable on any condition, second, that the gentleman would not discuss the affair with anyone, and third, that she would receive in advance the sum of five thousand pounds. The sum was enough to make many of the gentlemen blink and declare that no armful, no matter how attractive, was worth that sort of money.

But those who had thus far paid for and enjoyed the armful apparently had no complaints. When applied to for details, Brownlow sighed and shook his head, and would say no more than that she was an angel amongst women. Carteret refused to talk at all, saying a gentleman never discussed a lady, and Greville simply disappeared into Kent.

With this intelligence in his pocket, together with a fortune that could well stand the expenditure of five thousand pounds, or even double, come to that, Lord Dexter sought an interview with the lady. He saw her sitting alone at a rout a few days later and decided to make his play. He expressed his interest, said he was prepared to meet the terms he believed were required, and offered to succeed to the position of Bryce Greville.

Mrs. Ramsay regarded him with her clear grey eyes and said with a slight smile, "Oh? Are my terms so well known? I suppose I shouldn't be surprised. We women are held to be gossips, but I declare, gentlemen are worse."

"I assure you, dear Mrs. Ramsay," he had replied with some hauteur, "the gossip interests me only in as far as it enabled me to know...," he hesitated, "what I might expect. I find the terms very reasonable and, in fact, commend you on your business-like approach to what can often be a difficult subject."

"Thank you," she had replied, looking straight at him. "And thank you for your flattering attention, my lord, but the answer is *no*."

He was taken aback, for refusal was, as we have seen, something with which he was entirely unfamiliar. But his pride would not allow him to make any response than, "Very well. In that case we have nothing more to discuss. I wish you goodnight."

He bowed and left her sitting there.

His anger welling up inside, his lordship sought refuge in the cardroom. There, he proceeded to play with reckless abandon, winning and losing large sums with equal disregard. Some of his contemporaries had seen him talking to Mrs. Ramsay and one of them, a little more astute than the others, remarked, "I say, slow down Dexter! I collect she turned you down, but no need to take it out on us!"

"Turned you down? She didn't!"

There was general amazement, for Rory Compton was known to be a favorite with the ladies, even though his attentions were fleeting. Then as a newcomer entered, someone called out, "La Belle Ramsay has refused Dexter here, and he's playing like a madman. Best stay away!"

"But didn't you know, old fellow?" said the newcomer, ignoring the advice and sitting down backwards on one of the gold spindle-backed chairs so uncomfortable for playing cards but with which every hostess seemed to find it necessary to furnish the cardroom, "I hear she's already taken on Ferdy Carrington. At least, they were seen talking together and he's going about even more like someone who lost a shilling and found five pounds."

The Honorable Ferdinand Carrington was the younger son of a well-known family and would normally not have been able to afford Mrs. Ramsay's terms. For there was little money left in the family, and what there was would go to his older brother, the heir.

But an old uncle who had done very well on the 'Change had recently died and to everyone's surprise had left his fortune to Ferdinand. He'd done it, apparently, to spite his older brother, the Viscount, who had always looked down on him. The Viscount had the title and the encumbered family estate, but not much else. Ferdinand had declared himself happy as a grig. He had the money and none of the responsibilities. One of his first actions on learning of his inheritance had been to talk to Mrs. Ramsay.

Lord Dexter said nothing, but inside he was fuming. Why hadn't she said she'd already accepted someone else? And how had that whelp Carrington got there before him? Well, he was damned if he was going to wait another three months. Let her go. She'd pretty soon see she'd made a mistake.

He continued to play as recklessly as before, ending up several thousand pounds down and definitely more than a trifle castaway. Losing both the lady and the cards was an unusual event for him and he went home in the early hours, snapped at his butler and his valet, and fell unhappily into bed.

Over the next three months his lordship was seen with a different *inamorata* every other week. The *on-dit* was he was spending fabulous amounts at jewelers' establishment and it's certain that the ladies who had been seen on his arm subsequently appeared with extravagant parures that cast everyone else's into the shade. If he was hoping by these extravagances to attract the attention of one particular lady, he was singularly unsuccessful.

Mrs. Ramsay seemed not to notice either him or his companions, and her quiet elegance was such that no one would have thought her better looking had she been wearing expensive jewelry. In fact, she rarely wore anything more than a simple diamond pendant and matching earrings in the evenings, or pearls during the day. These were undoubtedly of the best quality, but hardly stunning.

A full two weeks before Carrington's period of protection was, by Lord Dexter's calculation, due to end, he renounced his own promise not to address her again, and sought another interview with the lady. It was at a ball, and when he was fairly sure all the waltzes had been taken, he asked to be placed on her card. He feigned disappointment when he was forced to settle for a country dance but in fact it had been a deliberate move.

When the time came, he sought her out and said with a bow, "As much as any dance with you, dear Mrs. Ramsay, must be a delight, I confess these country dances are not to my taste. One loses one's partner almost immediately and is forced to perform repetitive steps with every woman except the one with whom one desired to dance. May we therefore sit and enjoy each other's undivided attention?"

"Certainly, Lord Dexter," she replied calmly.

He led her to a sofa a little off to one side. The lady sat quietly, her hands in her lap, looking around the room with her small smile until, trying not to give any hint of the annoyance he was beginning to feel, he said, "I imagine you can have no doubt of my reason for wanting to talk to you."

"You are mistaken, my lord," she answered, looking guilelessly into his eyes. "I don't in the least know why you should wish to talk to me. In fact, I would have said you have quite deliberately not spoken to me these last months. But I'm sure you will enlighten me."

He was now positively annoyed. But it gave him some satisfaction to know she had noticed him not noticing her.

"Let's not play games, Mrs. Ramsay," he said. "I shall be blunt. I offered you my protection three months ago and you turned me down. I didn't know then, and you didn't enlighten me, that you had already entered into an arrangement with Carrington. But I believe that is soon to come to an end. I therefore repeat my offer."

"And I hope you will forgive me if I am equally blunt, my lord," she replied, still looking straight into his eyes. "I must make the same response as last time. Thank you for your attention, but the answer is no."

"What?" he cried, aghast. "You can't tell me you've already found someone else?"

"I don't believe I'm required to tell you anything, my lord," she said quietly, with complete composure. "I have thanked you for your offer, which I must refuse, and that is all I need to say."

"But why?" he was now too angry to control the level of his voice, and several people looked in their direction.

"I beg you to lower your voice, my lord. You will admit, I hope, that I am free to say yes or no, as I see fit. I don't feel compelled to give you an explanation. Now, if you will excuse me...."

She made as if to rise, but he took hold of her hand. "Compelled, be damned! You owe me an explanation. Is it money? I am prepared to pay you double what you usually ask. It is something else? Tell me what it is. I'm sure there's a solution." He realized he was begging, but he was too far gone to stop.

"Please, Lord Dexter. You are embarrassing yourself and me," she said softly. "I beg you let go of my hand and compose yourself. Let us sit here quietly for a moment so that people think there is nothing more to be seen."

He saw the sense in what she said and let go of her hand. They sat in silence watching the dancers. The country dance was nearing its end and they were both engaged for the next set. As the musicians made the final flourishes, his lordship stood. Anger and a sense of his own folly warred for ascendency in his breast, but it was no good. He knew his feelings would never change.

"Very well," he said quietly. "I shall not repeat my offer, but please know, Mrs. Ramsay, that it will always be open. And I pledge to be ever at your service, should you need me."

He kissed her hand and left her.

Chapter Ten

Hastings 1792

It had always been the plan that their stay in the inn was only temporary. The Rambuteaus would soon head for London, and there try to make contact with the other émigrés who had left France. In the end, though, two factors were responsible for their staying not a mile from where they had landed, in the village they soon learned was named Hastings.

The first was the weather. After the sunshine on the day of their landing, rain set in. It was April, after all. If it didn't rain all day, it certainly rained part of every day. It turned out that the best conveyance to London was the Mail coach from Dover. The Stage was also available, though it took longer.

But Dover was over fifty miles east of Hastings, and the only means they had of getting there was horse and cart. There was no covered conveyance available, even if they could have afforded it. In spite of his protestations, Claire absolutely rejected the idea of subjecting her husband to another day, or perhaps two, in the rain, followed by a minimum eight-hour coach ride to London. No, they would stay where they were until finer weather set in.

The second reason for their staying was Bernard's discovery that the local vicar, a handsome, kindly man, had an extensive library. He was the younger son of a good family with two older brothers and no hope of inheriting the estate, even had he wanted it. He therefore had the classic option of the Church or the Army.

His choice fell gratefully on the Church, for he was a man of little ambition other than to be left alone with his books. In truth, he was little interested in the lives of his parishioners, but his kindly demeanor and good looks made him a popular vicar. He and the Frenchman met when Bernard went out for a walk during a short gap between rainfalls and they were caught together sheltering in the church when the heavens opened up again. They quickly fell into conversation and discovered they were two of a kind.

An invitation to the vicarage soon followed. The vicar's wife was a charming lady who had had a number of much more advantageous offers upon her coming-out, but had fallen head over heels in love with the handsome young curate, as her husband then was. It was clear they were devoted to each other. Their rather ramshackle dwelling was overrun by two small boys and several large dogs.

They were soon on first name basis with Alice and Julian Beresford, and their twin boys Sebastian and Oliver, who were at the age justly named The Terrible Twos. Their door was thereafter always open to the French couple, often in the most literal sense, for the boys escaped their nanny as often as they could, and ran in and out with the dogs without it ever being closed. Whenever he was not at the inn, Claire knew her husband could be found in the library at the vicarage and she often walked over herself in the afternoons to take tea with the vicar's wife, who was fast becoming a friend.

Their English improved rapidly, both through conversation and though reading the books at their disposal. While for Bernard this was the extensive collection in the vicar's library, for Claire it was often the Romances that were discovered to be Alice's guilty pleasure.

"I know they're silly," said the vicar's wife, "but there's nothing like curling up with a good story, especially on a rainy day."

It was three months later as Claire sat in their bedchamber, contentedly refurbishing the baby clothes the vicar's wife had given her, the sun warm and the bees buzzing against the (now clean) mullioned windows, that she realized she was happy. No thought of going to London had crossed her mind for some weeks.

Life had settled into a pleasant routine. In the mornings she would help Agnès with the housework, though Agnès still constantly protested that such work was not fit for Madame. She should in any case relax for the sake of the baby. Nevertheless, some days Claire would walk into the village with Ivy. She learned where she could procure what they needed to live on: bread from the communal bakery, rabbits and pigeons from those who kept them, butter and cheese from the farmer's wife who brought them to the village once a week.

Claire's English became larded with Sussex expressions, which made her husband laugh. One day he heard her refer to the orchard as the *appleterre*, which was an odd combination he thought she had invented, but which turned out to be a local conflation of English and French, no doubt from the generations of trade between the two countries.

Joseph more or less took over as the general factotum of the inn. In the evenings he helped with bringing up the jugs of beer and cider from the cellar and even though at first he spoke no English at all, his size was sufficiently commanding to quell any fracas or show an over-imbiber the door.

During the day he chopped down dead trees from the orchard for the kitchen fire, and having discovered a much-neglected vegetable patch, set about bringing it back into production. It was a mystery how he did it, but he managed to procure seedlings from the inn's regular customers and as the weeks passed, a profusion of vegetables began to unfurl their green shoots.

Agnès, aided by Claire when she permitted it, which was not often, took over the housework and the kitchen, where she became undisputed ruler, as she had in Paris. After a few weeks, the place was clean, the upstairs free of fleas and the downstairs clear of spiders' webs and mouse nests. The kitchen was unrecognizable. Woe betide anyone tracking in mud from the back door!

The chief culprit was the landlord, Josiah Parrish, the only unwashed thing left in the house. His excursions outside were almost exclusively to the privy and his favorite spot in the hedge. But Agnès would stand at the back door awaiting his return, her hands on her hips and the glint in her black eyes. She would bar the way in until he had wiped his boots on the straw she put down for the purpose. Neither of them could speak the other's language, but he knew when he was beaten. He became so used to doing it that finally he wiped his boots without being told to do so.

Nor did he long remain the only unclean thing in the place. One fine morning Agnès approached Ivy and gave her to understand she wanted all her husband's clothing. Pots of hot water were ready to wash it and him. They both stole upstairs and while he snorted in an alcoholic haze, slowly and gently stripped him off. Agnès turned her eyes away in the last stages, less for modesty's sake than because Josiah was a truly disgusting sight, his white flesh hanging loosely from his body. Holding the odiferous items at arm's length, the two women took them downstairs and plunged what they could into boiling water. The woolens they took outside and lay in the damp grass. They would hang them up to dry and brush later.

An hour or so later there was a roar from upstairs. "What the... where's my bloody britches and my...?" They could hear a frantic stamping and then boots on the wooden steps. Josiah appeared wrapped in a blanket, his boots on his feet.

"There," said his wife, gesturing towards the back garden. "There's your britches and the rest. We washed 'em. Yer lucky. It were a toss-up between that and the bonfire, they was that stinking. Now, we've brung in the old tub and you're to 'ave a good wash yourself. You do it, or I'll get Joseph to 'old you down and Agnes and me, we'll do it for yer. That's if yer want 'er seein' yer parts."

Josiah eyed his wife and then Agnès. His wife he could deal with, but the Frenchwoman, she scared him, so she did, with her black eyes and her glare. So the women poured hot water into the tub and added cold until it was just warm. Agnès left as Ivy was saying, "Go on, get in yer big baby. I'll scrub yer back."

She sat in the main room and for a while could hear vociferous grumbling and complaints, till it grew silent and sounds of a different sort arose.

Sometime later Ivy emerged, looking a little sheepish but with a faint smile on her lips. Agnès wondered that any woman could find such a man in the least attractive. But, she said to herself, *à chacun son goût* (each to his own taste).

Chapter Eleven

Hastings 1792

Bernard did his best to help Joseph. Physical labor had never been his forte, but he was willing to learn. Joseph taught him how to handle a spade and chop wood. He was now proud of the callouses on his previously soft scholar's hands. Then one day he discovered a book in the vicar's library describing the edible plants of Kent and offering recipes for using them. Thus he read about sloe gin, blackberry wine, cider-making and, of course, producing beer from the hops that grew wild everywhere. The casks in the cellar were almost empty and they had little confidence in Josiah's ability or desire to teach them what they needed to know to replenish them. Learning how to make home-brew was their next challenge.

Between what Ivy and Claire purchased and what Joseph grew in his garden, Agnès produced delicious meals. By late afternoon the inn would smell wonderfully of whatever she was cooking. Customers coming in would sniff appreciatively and it wasn't long before she began serving dinner to those who arrived early enough for there to be any left. She was soon preparing enough to feed a small army. The money earned that way was used to buy food supplies and the rest was passed on to Ivy. The landlady was delighted. Though Josiah still did nothing but eat food he had in no way helped to procure, drank himself into a stupor most nights and had to be forced to clean himself up from time to time, as far as she was concerned, life at the inn was better than it had been for a long time.

Claire approached the vicar's wife about selling the silver they had brought with them. Her new friend laughed delightedly at the story of how it had been hidden in sacks of manure and directed her to a dealer she had herself done business with. She had once wanted to sell a piece of jewelry in order to buy her husband a rare book he had set his heart upon. The business was completed to everyone's satisfaction and Claire was now fairly plump in the pocket. She left her jewelry in the hem of her cloak. Perhaps she would have a daughter who would one day marry a rich man and wear them at her wedding… she allowed herself to dream.

So as she sat happily sewing in the bedchamber, Claire came to a conclusion. That night she and Bernard had a quiet conversation as they lay in bed.

"Chéri," she said, "are you happy here?"

"I'm happy anywhere I'm with you, and our little one," he replied, caressing her swollen midsection.

"Because I know we had planned to go on to London, but I've been thinking. What would you do there? How would we live? Why don't we just stay here? To be sure, it's not what either of us was born to, but we have a livelihood, and we have friends. Who knows what it would be like in the city?"

"But can we find a good *accoucheur* for the baby?" Bernard sounded worried.

"The women here have babies! They must know of someone. I'll ask Alice."

"If that's what you want, it's what I want, my love. I've told you before," said her husband, wrapping his arms around her, "You're always right!"

"We must talk to Agnès and Joseph. We could not manage here without them, so if they want to go, we must go too."

And that's what she told them the next day. Agnès was astonished that Monsieur and Madame would plan their whole future around what she and her husband wanted.

"It's not for us to say where we go and what we do," she said stoutly. "It's our duty to follow you, and we will. Whatever you want, Madame. Not to say," she added after a moment, looking around, "that I wouldn't be glad enough to stay here now the place is looking more like what we're used to and I've got my kitchen up to snuff. What d'you say, Joseph?"

"I says a man is happy when his woman's happy. So if you wants it, I wants it. Besides, the cabbage and pumpkins is doing a treat, we've been drying the hops to make beer and I'm looking at them apples and thinking Calvados. If Monsieur can find a book what gives us the how-to."

"Calvados?" said Bernard. "Now there's an idea! I doubt an English book would have Calvados exactly, but I might find one with information on how to distill other liquors, and I imagine it would be about the same."

"Then if Ivy agrees, it's settled," said Claire. "We shall become English innkeepers with French food and Calvados. We shall be famous throughout the land!"

Ivy, who had not been looking forward to the French visitors leaving, readily agreed to continue the arrangement they had.

Over the next years, if they did not become famous throughout the land, they did develop a local reputation for the excellence of their kitchen and their alcohol. It helped them that Hastings grew from a village to a town as it began to cater for the wealthy summer visitors who, because of the rampages of Bonaparte across Europe, were now coming to the south coast instead of going to the Continent. The Prince Regent set the fashion in Brighton and visitors overflowed into Hastings. A Parade, or seafront promenade, was built and rebuilt as the unforgiving elements battered it. Wealthy families rented the new homes built along the seafront.

Agnes went on cooking, bringing a French flair to pigeon pie, mutton, and rabbit stew. Her sole fried in brown butter with lemon was a triumph, and her dish featuring the local cod in butter and cream was sold out almost as soon as it was ready. She smoked herring and mackerel. Bernard and Joseph made homebrew and cider with the very able help of Ivy who had for years assisted Josiah. The exterior of the inn was repaired and repainted. But what really set them apart in the end was the Calvados.

It was a labor of love and trust. Bernard was able to obtain a book called *The Art of Distillation* published by John French in 1651. He and Joseph made the arduous journey to London to procure the equipment needed. They came back saying thank God they didn't live up there with the noise and the smoke. They were glad to be out of it. That first September they set aside some of the crushed apple mush fermenting for cider. They left it till fermentation had ceased and then heated it in a special boiler with a cap that collected the distillate. The process took days and required a great deal of heat. Much to Agnès' disgust they did it in one corner of the kitchen fire, staying up all night to tend it.

The whole house smelled of apples and alcohol, and the customers asked what was going on. The liquor was stored in one of the empty cider casks. It tasted very harsh, but they knew it had to mature. For the next two Septembers they repeated the process and by the third, when they tasted the first cask it was declared as close to Calvados as could be expected from English apples, made in an English inn.

In the golden October of that first year Claire was delivered of a daughter. She was attended by the local midwife, who had assisted at the birth of all the children in the village and most of their parents too. The vicar and his wife gladly agreed to be her godparents and she was christened into the Church of England, though her parents were, of course, Catholic. They called her Héloise.

Chapter Twelve

London 1816

Héloise Ramsay closed the door behind her lover and leaned against it, breathing a sigh of relief. It had, as always, been difficult persuading him that his time was up. Why was it that men would willingly agree to her terms and then try to alter them at the last moment? She knew the sum she asked was exorbitant by any standard, and she had chosen it precisely because she thought it was simply too much for them to repeat. But inevitably they tried to do so, and after trying everything else, she would just have to tell them she didn't want them anymore. She was as kind as she could be, but that was the plain fact. She didn't say, of course, that she hadn't wanted them in the first place. That she had accepted them for that very reason. She never accepted a *carte blanche* from anyone she was in any way attracted to. She knew better.

Now she was free for a couple of weeks! She always gave herself that respite before her next engagement. She usually went down to Hastings to see her family. She would slip on her old clothes and take the Mail, which now ran to Hastings. She would spend a week at the inn, telling Maman about her life, inventing stories for Agnès and Joseph, eating good food, and sleeping in her old bedroom under the quilt Maman had made her. After the deceptions of London, it was balm to her soul.

She walked slowly into her drawing room. It was charming. The windows, chairs and sofas were covered in straw-colored silk and there were water color scenes on the walls. On the floor lay a large pale blue Aubusson rug with a floral medallion. The room was saved from being overly feminine by the size and style of the furniture. This was large and comfortable; a man might sink into an armchair without fear of spindly legs cracking beneath his weight, or lie back on a sofa without the sense it might fall over with him in it. Added to this, there were newspapers and books lying about, so it gave a lived-in feeling, not the impression of a parlor reserved for visitors.

The room ran from the front to the back of the tiny townhouse just on the edges of fashionable Mayfair. There were tall French windows leading out onto a paved courtyard in the back. This was enclosed by a high brick wall over which climbing roses and Virginia creeper tumbled in mixed profusion. In the late spring and summer the color and perfume of roses overtook all, but when they ceased blooming, Héloise donned thick gloves and ruthlessly pruned them back. She had learned from Joseph that for plants and trees to flourish they had to be kept under control.

"See, Mademoiselle Héloise," he told her once, pruning the apple trees in their orchard, "a tree is like a man. Its heart is only so big. If it gets too big and heavy the heart gives out. Just like old Josiah."

She could remember Josiah Parrish, the original owner of the inn where she'd been brought up. She never saw him doing anything other than sit in the corner and eat Agnès' good food with a full glass in front of him. He had never been unkind to her, but he smelled bad and she didn't like him. He had become so heavy he could hardly get to his feet and go out to the privy. Agnès told her that's why he stank.

When she was five, he had been found one morning, lifeless and cold, his body on the landing and his legs on the top stairs. Her father had told her the man's heart had given out. The men had buried him in the churchyard and when she and Agnès and her mother went to see the place where he lay (for women did not go to burial services) they saw Joseph there. He showed Héloïse how he had spliced a branch of one of their orchard apples onto a crab apple growing wild at the foot of the grave.

"In a few years there'll be good apples on this old tree," he said. "I hopes the angels makes cider fer him. He always liked 'is jug."

"Will the angels make cider, maman?" Héloïse had asked.

"No, chérie," replied her mother. "That's just Joseph's joke. But the apple blossom will be pretty in the spring."

A month later Ivy told them she wanted to leave the inn and go to live with her daughter in London. By now she had three young children and needed the help. The Rambuteaus had grown fond of the crusty old lady, and, in her own way, she of them. She loved Héloïse like a granddaughter but, as she said to Claire, her real grandchildren needed her, and blood was blood.

They had lived frugally the last five years, putting most of the money they earned back into the inn to make it suitable for the wealthier customers who came in the summer months. They had managed to put by a small sum of money, to which Claire added what was left from the sale of the silver brought over from France on that dreadful crossing. They gave half of it all to Ivy. Bernard wrote out a bill of sale transferring ownership of the inn. Ivy carefully wrote her name and the vicar witnessed it. She had never expected such generosity and was astonished at being paid what seemed to her a fabulous sum. She said she would have simply given them the property, but the Rambuteaus insisted on paying what they could, declaring she had quite literally saved their lives.

There were tears at her departure, but after all, a sense of relief. The place was now their own. As Claire had said, they were English innkeepers. Joseph took down the worn old sign hanging over the front door and Bernard repainted it. It read: The *Traveller's Rest. Props: Rambuteau & Thomas.* Agnès and Joseph were speechless.

"But Monsieur!" protested Agnès. "It's not fitting, our name next to yours!"

"Most certainly it is. We could not run this place without you two. It belongs to you as much as to us. Remember: liberty, equality, fraternity. We are the embodiment of the Revolution. Look!"

And he showed where the bill of sale, duly witnessed by the vicar, named as equal partners Bernard and Claire Rambuteau and Joseph and Agnès Thomas.

Agnès, who never cried, burst into tears and Joseph, red around the ears, looked at the floor, shuffled his feet, and finally wrung Bernard's hand.

"Merci, Monsieur," was all he could trust himself to say.

But Joseph and Agnès could never forget that their relationship had always been that of servant and master. They protested they could never call Claire and Bernard by their first names, Revolution or no Revolution, so Monsieur and Madame they remained. Héloise was always Mademoiselle.

Héloise had only been five at the time, but she could remember it all clearly. In fact, it seemed to her it was the moment her life began.

Chapter Thirteen

Hastings 1797

The first change in Héloise's life after her parents became owners of the inn was that she was given her own room. Up till then she had slept in a trundle bed in the corner of her parents' room. But now they had two free rooms. Ivy's was a fairly large chamber on the front and Josiah's a small one at the back. Ivy had years ago grown tired of having her intoxicated husband fall upon her in the early hours and had started locking her chamber door. Josiah would then stumble into the next closest bed until Agnès had taken the precaution of locking the doors to the two good rooms furnished with new mattresses and linen for visitors. Josiah was ultimately forced into the small back room, but as he was always drunk when he went to bed, he hardly noticed. His small room was chosen to become Héloise's. The larger room would be used for more overnight guests.

Joseph had taken to whitewashing the trunks of the apple trees every year. He used a compound of slaked lime and water mixed with egg white to help it stick. It supposedly kept them cool and prevented too-early budding. He now made up some of the mixture to paint the walls of Héloise's little bedroom. Its fresh smell and appearance went a long way to eliminating the *parfum de Josiah* as Claire delicately called it. Joseph also fashioned hooks from apple branches for her clothes, and when Alice, the vicar's wife, heard her godchild was getting her own room, she gave her a mirror from the vicarage.

Claire had bought some blue and white ticking from a French peddler who had made his way along the coast a few months before. It surprised the French family that these peddlers still came, considering the bad relationship between France and Britain during the last several years. People from Dover had reported they knew the French troops were exercising on the sands of Calais because from the top of the white cliffs behind the town they could see the sun flashing on their sabers.

Nevertheless, the ancient trade between the two countries persisted. Some was clandestine: up and down the coast Kentish and Sussex smugglers had hidden troves of imported French brandy on which no tax would ever be paid. But much of it, like the peddlers, was straightforward. In the summer they would cross from France and walk down the roads of southern England, stopping in all the villages and inns along the way. Their carts were bedecked with ribbons, lace, fabrics and other more prosaic items like pots and pans, onions and garlic.

The first time one stopped by *The Traveller's Rest*, they were all charmed, not only by his wares but even more by the chance to get news from home. The man was so besieged with offers of food and drink that he felt like visiting royalty, and gladly spent the afternoon with his countrymen who were, as he saw it, marooned *chez les Rosbif* . They had seen him again, and others, in subsequent years. Claire bought fabrics and trim for the women's gowns and men's shirts and had recently picked up the length of blue and white ticking. This was a very closely woven cotton made in Nîmes in southern France, perfect for mattress covers, as the quills of duck feathers couldn't poke through.

After discussion of the relative merits of emptying Josiah's old mattress of its feathers, washing the covering and attempting to remove the *parfum de Josiah* from the whole, Claire and Agnès decided to burn it all. They couldn't bear the idea, they said, of their little girl sleeping on anything that had once born the body of that stinking old man. They paid a farmer's wife for duck feathers and made Héloise a new mattress using the Nîmes ticking. Like everyone else, she would have a wood frame bed with ropes tied across to suspend the mattress. Joseph fashioned a wooden armchair and with scraps of fabric from worn out garments, her mother made her patchwork curtains and a pad for her chair.

Héloise felt like a queen in her new room. As she grew older, she would sit by the window reading, most often the romance novels from the vicar's wife. Her room overlooked the orchard at the back and in the spring, with the apple blossom like snow and its scent in her nose, she sometimes felt as if she were in heaven, like one of the angels Joseph had talked about.

Thinking about it now as she stood looking into her back-garden haven in the city, she knew she had enjoyed a charmed childhood. Everyone loved her, watched over her and gave her what they could. If she never had a dress that wasn't made from someone's old gown, and the only doll she ever possessed was made by Joseph from a knot of apple wood, clad in a piece of fabric from her third-hand baby gown, she had been happy.

The second way her life had changed when her parents bought the inn was that her formal education had begun. Her parents had always spoken to her in both languages, but naturally her French was stronger than her English. Her mother now began early to teach her to read and write in their own tongue. This was just as well, for though Joseph's English became fairly good,

Agnès found their adopted language barbarous from beginning to end, and could never get much beyond her initial *Verray will zank yew*. She understood well enough though, and between using her fingers to indicate numbers and pointing at what she wanted, could do the marketing with amazing success. The locals knew it was useless to try to cheat the Frenchwoman who had eyes like the devil and a temper to go with them.

Mademoiselle Héloise was the only person who was allowed free range in her kitchen. Agnès fed her tidbits and chattered with her all day long. She would take her on her knee and sing her the traditional songs of her own childhood: *au clair de la lune, petit matelot* (and she would tell her how her Maman and Papa came across the sea to find her in England), and *Alouette*. This last she would often sing while preparing pigeons for her famous pies and suit the action to the song, plucking the head, the neck, and the back of the bird. Héloise found it highly amusing and would skip around the kitchen singing with her as the feathers flew.

But her mother and father had decided from the outset that their daughter must grow up as an English lady, and as an education for an English lady it clearly wasn't sufficient. Luckily, their friend Alice taught her two sons, and declared herself ready to give Héloise her first English lessons. The boys were by now eight years old and had progressed onto the more rigorous teaching of their father, who was preparing them for Eton.

For the next two years the girl learned her English ABC's with the vicar's wife. She was clever and learned fast, so that by the time she was seven, Alice declared she was ready to continue with her husband and sons. Thereafter, Héloise sat with the twins, absorbing geography, history, and elementary Latin like a sponge. By the time they were due to go to Eton, she was at the same level as they, for apart from being very bright, unlike them, she studied her books. They were more interested in cricket than verb conjugations.

When the twins left for Eton, the vicar was more than happy to continue giving Héloise lessons in the classic English school curriculum, and if her lessons were often interrupted by his darting up from his seat and searching for a volume he knew he had somewhere, in which they would find the perfect illustration of the point he had been making, she was none the worse for that. At the same time, she and her father studied French seriously, using the only French book they had: Rousseau's *La Nouvelle Héloïse*. There was a great deal she didn't understand at first, but her father was patient and she was a good student. Besides, she very much identified with her namesake in the book.

Now Héloise gave a little sigh. How lucky she had been! How many girls had two gentle scholars leading her studies? How could anyone have foreseen her life turning out how it had? She recalled sitting in the vicar's book-lined study talking about Caesar's Gallic Wars. Though she had never been to France, she had inherited a fierce loyalty to her parents' homeland and was affronted to find that Caesar had found the Gauls crude and shiftless, overly inclined to violence and speaking a language he found ugly. This view contrasted vividly with the elegance of mind demonstrated by Héloise in the book she re-read constantly with her father. She thus learned very early that truth was a matter of perspective. It was a lesson she would return to later.

Chapter Fourteen

London 1816

Héloise now sat in her charming London drawing room and found herself thinking about Rory Dexter. How hard it had been to refuse him that last time! In fact, she'd been amazed he'd sought her out again. She was fairly sure he'd been flaunting those other women in front of her, and it had taken all her willpower to appear calm and uninterested. Then he'd offered twice her usual rate! For a moment, she'd been tempted, but she had fiercely tamped down her desire. She knew only too well where that road led!

The front door knocker sounded suddenly in the little Mayfair home and woke her from her reverie. She kept a staff of only two: a husband and wife team who were so discreet as to be almost invisible. She never had visitors other than her current lover, and to these she opened the door herself. She did so now, and was shocked to find herself confronted by the person of Sebastian, one of the vicarage twins she had grown up with. He had completed his studies and, to the distress of his gentle parents, gone into the Army. His brother had followed in his father' footsteps and was vicar at a country parish in Hertfordshire. Sebastian was dressed in full regimentals and looked extremely handsome.

"Héloise!" he exclaimed. "It *is* you. I thought it was, but when they said...."

"Sebastian!" she threw her arms around his neck, then realized they were still on the doorstep. Her neighbors already looked at her askance; they knew what she was. But no need to give them more to gossip about.

"Don't stand talking on the doorstep!" she said. "Won't you come in?"

Her visitor looked around a little abashed, for he too knew what she was.

"It's Major Beresford now," he said. "I don't know if I should come in, as a matter of fact. I wouldn't want anyone to think...."

"You were visiting a well-known courtesan," completed Héloise. "I know. I don't think anyone has seen you so far but if you keep standing on the doorstep, they might. Anyway, you'll be glad to know I'm *such* an expensive consort, being seen with me will raise your standing no end in the clubs!"

She led a reluctant Sebastian into the living room, where the French doors still stood open to the late afternoon sun and the autumn gold of the Virginia creeper cast its warm glow. Her visitor looked around appreciatively.

"I say! This is something like!" Then he rethought himself. "Oh, I suppose it's part of your... trade."

Héloise laughed. "Well, yes, it is! My gentlemen like to be comfortable, after all!"

"But why, Héloise? Why?" he asked plaintively. "I arrived in town on furlough for a few weeks and I couldn't believe what I heard in my club. They were talking about how Bromsey was a lucky devil to get Mrs. Ramsay next. I asked what they meant, and they told me Héloise Ramsay was the hottest thing in town these days, if you could afford her. So I asked what was so special about her. They said she was tall and beautiful, with brown curls and grey eyes, and spoke French like Marie Antoinette. She was very cultured and every inch a lady except she was available… for a price. And what a price! Well, the description sounded just like you and Héloise isn't a very common name. Ramsay isn't unlike Rambuteau, so I just put it together. But why, Héloise," he repeated, "why?"

"The money, Sebastian," she said simply. "We need the money. But please, please don't tell anyone you know me!"

Chapter Fifteen

Hastings 1803

The Rambuteaus' good friend the vicar came from a well-established and prosperous family with an estate in Hertfordshire. As the youngest son, he had no expectations of inheriting the family estate and fortune. But he had a small jointure, allowing him to live comfortably on his earnings as a village parson. He had an older sister, as good-looking as he in appearance, but as unlike him in character as may be imagined. She was as hard-headed as he was dreamy. Even at sixteen, she had been a most decided maiden of a practical disposition.

She made up her mind as a very young woman to marry into the peerage. This would give her, she knew, the influence and position she wanted. Luckily, she was an accredited beauty in her day, and fixed her eye on the wealthy Lord Pevensey in her first season. He was more than ten years her senior and had escaped marriage those many years. But determination was her middle name. What she wanted, she made a play for, and what she made a play for, she won. Before he knew it, Lord Pevensey had a pretty young wife who ordered him and his whole household better than it had ever been ordered before.

She gained for herself an unassailable position in the *ton* by holding parties to which all the highest in the land would come. They were sure of good food and drink and none of the silly games some hostesses thrust upon them. Instead, on offer were a few good rounds of whist for sometimes very high stakes, the hostess herself becoming a formidable opponent. She knew, however, when to win and when to lose, so that no one ever went away feeling he or she had been fleeced by her ladyship. On the contrary, guests often left plumper in the pocket and well satisfied with themselves.

Lady Pevensey was fond of her younger brother and would visit him occasionally. She would descend on the ramshackle vicarage where the servants generally took full advantage of the relaxed housekeeping of their employers, and she would send them scurrying in all directions. She would scold both them and him, trying to encourage her brother to be more forceful.

"He is a dear," she would say to Alice, "but you need to keep him up to snuff. He hasn't the sense of a babe."

Alice adored her handsome husband and in her eyes he could do no wrong, even when the sexton would come hurrying up to the house to remind him he had a burial to attend and all the mourners had been standing half an hour in the churchyard, or when money went missing from the collection plate and suspicion fell on any number of perfectly innocent people until it was found unaccountably rolled up in his crumpled surplice. She was used to her formidable sister-in-law. When she tried to change their ways, Alice simply mumbled something non-committal. She and her husband both liked and admired her ladyship, but always heaved a sigh of relief when she left.

One year, when Héloise was about eleven, both Lord and Lady Pevensey stopped at the vicarage on their way to Dover and a trip across the channel. Hostilities between the two countries were momentarily suspended and like many ladies of the *ton*, Lady Pevensey was going to Paris to shop. It was April, and the weather notoriously fickle. Their trip from London had begun in sunshine, but ended in a chilly drizzle. Carriages were most often left in Dover, to be picked up on the return trip. Rented vehicles were available in Calais. The Pevenseys were therefore taking just the one carriage to Dover. It was loaded with her ladyship, her maid, and a quantity of luggage, while his lordship's valet and Lord Pevensey himself, by now a man in his sixties, had ridden alongside. When the rain came on as they crossed the Downs, they were both drenched.

His lordship had been told of the Calvados now offered at *The Traveller's Rest* and, still feeling a chill in his bones, the following morning he decided to take advantage of what promised to be fine weather by walking down there to try a glass. His wife was in the cellar, checking on the record of wine consumption (she suspected the staff of tippling), or she would have probably stopped him. The vicar and his wife just nodded absently when he proposed the walk. He was thinking about his sermon and she was reading a letter they had received from the boys at Eton. So he wandered off to *The Traveller's Rest* and enjoyed a glass or two of the Calvados and a chat with Bernard. Then he set off back to the vicarage. The sky had darkened in the meantime and soon after he left, the heavens opened up and he was drenched for the second day running.

Chapter Sixteen

Hastings 1803

Lord Pevensey arrived back at the vicarage with no one to greet him. His wife had dragged her poor brother and his wife into the kitchen to give the servants a piece of his (or rather, her) mind. This the vicar was doing both unhappily and ineffectually. His lordship's valet and her ladyship's dresser were also downstairs covertly listening to the goings-on, with the natural superiority of the London servant over their country counterparts. The bell ropes were broken, so no one heard his summons for help. The miserably wet peer, who had never looked after himself in his life, sat shivering before an inadequate fire in the drawing room until his wife found him there nearly an hour later.

The poor man was then harangued for being so foolish and bundled upstairs. But in spite of a hot mustard bath for his feet, a warm brick in his bed and servings of hot broth, he succumbed to a dreadful cold. When this turned to an inflammation of the lungs, Alice sent for her friend Claire.

Over the years, Claire had more than once had recourse to the cupping treatment she had seen old Madeleine use on her husband on their way to Calais all that time ago. She remembered the name of the plant the woman had used to make her oil and tisane and when Bernard had found that old book of the plants and flora of the region, she had been able to identify it. Luckily the French word was very close to the English: hyssop. She found the pretty blue plant when it bloomed in the midsummer of their first year and experimented making tea with the leaves. It was not unpleasant, with a faint aniseed flavor.

She had no idea how to make the oil, but after a deal of trial and error she discovered how to distill it from the leaves and stalks of the plant. One placed the mashed green part of the plant into a pan of water with a dry basin in the center. The water in the pan had to be low enough not to overflow into the basin when it boiled. The lid of the pan was placed upside down over it all, and as the water began to boil inside the pan, cold water had to be added to the concave center of the lid on top. This caused the evaporated liquor to condense on the underside of the lid and drip into the basin. It was a long and tricky process but at length produced enough distillate to fill a bottle. This had to be capped and kept cool so that the oil settled on the top and could be carefully poured off. She could use the oil as it was, but the production of it was so lengthy and difficult that to make it go further, she practiced mixing it with small quantities of beeswax, obtainable in the village. This made a salve. The rest of the distilled liquor could be drunk as a hot tea.

The first winter they were in Hastings, they had been careful to keep Bernard from the damp. He had been forbidden to go out in the rain and was made to stay by the fire the minute Claire thought he might be chilled. This worked so well that the second winter Bernard thought he was cured of his lung condition and proceeded to dig up vegetables in the rain. The result was a recurrence of the inflammation of the lungs. Luckily, by that time

Claire had worked out how to make the hyssop oil salve and was able to use it as Madeleine had done. When she sold their silver, she had the foresight to keep back the silver wine cups they had brought from Paris. Using these, she imitated the old woman's cupping method and was able to treat her husband successfully.

She now brought her salve and silver cups to the vicarage and administered to Lord Pevensey. The unfortunate peer was very poorly, his breathing shallow and labored. The cupping helped to arrest the progress of the inflammation but it was many days before he could breathe with anything like ease.

Lady Pevensey genuinely loved her husband but with her hectoring manner proved herself so poor a nurse that in the end, Alice and Claire had to forbid her to enter her husband's room. She instead patrolled the vicarage, finding fault with everything and everyone. The twins were luckily away at Eton and saved from her not-so-tender ministrations, but it took all the poor vicar's patience and charity to deal with a sister whose own unhappiness could only find relief in making everyone else equally miserable.

When, at length, Lord Pevensey's health began to make significant strides forward, it was Héloise who entertained him as he sat bundled in blankets by the fire. Her parents were too busy, the vicar too preoccupied, and his wife too impatient. At eleven she was tall and slender to the point of thinness, with no hint of the curves she would later develop. She wore her hair in simple braids down her back.

She had no sense of herself as a woman and was utterly uninterested in any of the domestic arts. When the twins were away at school she preferred working with Joseph in the garden, and when they came home would follow them along, begging to be included in any physical activity they might suggest, from climbing trees for birds' nests to leaping over streams swollen by the spring rain, and falling in as often as they.

Now she settled herself down with his lordship and began to do the only non-physical thing she knew how to do: read alternately in French and English. She read to him from the newspaper or from the English books she had studied with the vicar and from the only French one she had. Lord Pevensey was entranced by this young person, no more than a girl, who was equally at home in both languages and could enter into an intelligent discussion with him, just as she did with both her teachers.

She would read him a passage in French and, if necessary, paraphrase it into English. Like most of the aristocracy, his lordship knew some French. In spite of the long-standing enmity between the two counties, the upper classes of both had always learned each other's language. He listened with pleasure to Héloise's clear voice reading her native tongue, but discussed the implications of what he heard with her in English.

He had a wry sense of humor that was usually lost beneath his wife's more strident pronouncements. Rousseau was hardly a humorist, but Lord Pevensey had a way of looking at things that made Héloise laugh unaffectedly, and he would chuckle with her. Her ladyship would hear them and poke her head around the door, saying, "I can't imagine what you both find so amusing. There's so much that needs to be *done*!" But she would leave to supervise the turning out of another cupboard or the acquisition of new linens, smiling that her husband, about whom she had been seriously worried, was feeling so much better.

The noble couple abandoned the trip to Paris and returned home a few weeks later. When they left, Lady Pevensey clasped Héloise's hand and said, "You're a good girl! When you are a little older, you must come to stay with us in London."

A lady married to a peer of the realm inviting the landlady's daughter, said Bernard afterwards, now that was the Revolution in action! Héloise's mother looked at it differently. She saw the invitation as a much hoped-for entrée into polite society for the daughter she was trying, in spite of their circumstances, to raise as a lady.

In fact, Héloise never went to visit the noble couple in London while Lord Pevensey was still alive. He died two years later, not as the consequences of a lung condition, but by being run down in the street. A clap of thunder had panicked a team of spirited horses and their driver, an exquisite in yellow pantaloons and a striped coat, had been unable to control them. His lordship had just stepped into the road to retrieve his hat, swept off his head by a wild gust of wind that had accompanied the thunder, and was mown down by the careening horses.

Lady Pevensey was broken-hearted and for a while became almost a recluse. She stopped entertaining and even after her long period of mourning contented herself with small, very select, card parties. In this way, though she rarely went out, she still kept her finger on the pulse of the *ton*, knew everyone and was generally regarded as the doyenne of the older set. When Héloise re-entered her life, it was to be under very different circumstances.

Chapter Seventeen

Hastings 1807-1808

By the time she was fifteen, Héloise's thinness had been replaced by curves, and while she was still slim, she was developing a beautiful figure. She still braided her hair but now the plaits wound around her head and chestnut curls escaped to cluster at her temples and at the nape of her neck. She had wide grey eyes and a beautiful complexion. Her education had made her serious beyond her years, but her imagination was full of the romantic notions she had grown up with. It was now she, rather than her mother, who would spend afternoons with the vicar's wife, talking about the novels of Ann Radcliffe. They had read them all, from *The Castles of Athlin and Dunbayne* and the *Romance of the Forest* to *The Mysteries of Udolpho* and *The Italian.*

It was not surprising that a young woman who had been practically weaned on *The New Héloise* should find much to admire in these novels of mystery, terror, and romance. In both cases, the heroines were strong women who clung to their love in spite of the obstacles they faced, fearless and alone. Rousseau, no less than the writers of the gothic novels, gave his female character a fearlessness of spirit and faith in the power of love.

Though she was surrounded by adults who loved and protected her, Héloise was often alone. In her desire to bring up her daughter as a lady, Claire had discouraged her from forming friendships with the other young women of the village. By now, she had nothing in common with them. At fifteen they were usually "walking out" with the boys who would become their husbands. By sixteen they were often married and even starting their families. She rarely went further afield than to the vicarage, so that though she had been brought up in the country, Héloise had no knowledge of farming or the animals who might have been a crude introduction to the act of procreation. Carefully shielded from these realities, she knew nothing at all of the physical relations between men and women.

The vicarage twins were now at university and she saw them less and less frequently. They preferred to spend the breaks with friends rather than come home where there was little more to do than hunting rabbits or going fishing. A couple of the sons of farming families would have paid court to her if she had ever noticed them. But how could she be interested in a boy in a coarse woolen coat and britches, a checkered cloth around his neck, a dirty cap on his head, as often as not carrying a dead rabbit or birds shot with the rifle he carried under his arm, when she had read about poets in black-tailed coats and white linen reading passionate lines to their loves?

Nor was she allowed to serve in the inn. Claire deemed the local men unfit company for her daughter. She made her keep to the kitchen, but Agnès would not let her cook, so Héloise was most often to be found in her bedchamber, where she re-read her books or dreamed her time away. Surrounded by love, she was nevertheless lonely.

One day, shortly before her sixteenth birthday, she was shopping in the village when a stranger on a fine black horse stopped to ask the way to the inn. He had been staying some miles away and had heard about the Calvados. If he was struck by her pretty face and even more by her ripening figure, she was open-mouthed at the man she saw before her. He was an almost perfect representation of the hero of her Romances. He jumped down from his shining black steed and stood before her in an elegant riding jacket and close-fitting pale-colored pantaloons covered to the knee by shining top boots, a gleaming white neckcloth, and a tall, smooth hat on his head.

"If you just keep going through the village, sir, you will see the inn." Then she added with a blush, "I have a few items to purchase, but if you don't mind waiting, I will show you the way. I live there, you see."

"Then please allow me to accompany you as you shop, fair maiden," he replied, responding to her refined accent with an old-fashioned courtesy that might have sounded laughable to anyone more worldly, but which to Héloise was perfectly romantic. He had noticed the blush and heard her voice. He was surprised to hear she lived at the inn. He had judged her to be the product of a young ladies' Academy, highly protected and with little or no experience of gentlemen.

He took her basket in one hand and his horse's bridle in the other, and walked beside her around the village as she bought the items Agnès had put on her list. She led him at length to the inn, but declined to go in with him, saying, "My mother doesn't like me to be in the saloon, sir."

"And she is right, fair one, she is right," answered her cavalier. "No one who looks like you should be seen in such a place, nor should your foot touch the sullied ground."

Héloise looked down at her serviceable boots, muddy from the walk through the village. "I'm afraid they've already done that!" she smiled up at him. "But what you said was very pretty."

"Upon my life, no prettier than you," the gentleman answered promptly. "But if you cannot go in, then neither shall I. Won't you dispose of this," he gestured with the basket, "and let us go for a walk. I shall count it the best day of my life to walk down a country lane with an angel."

Like all young women throughout all ages, Héloise had been taught not to walk off with strange men. But it didn't count when it was noon on a fair autumn day and the man was as handsome and poetic as this one. So she ran lightly to the back door of *The Traveller's Rest* and gave the provisions to Agnès. Agnès was involved in skinning a rabbit and paid no attention when she ran off again.

And thus began a courtship that seemed like a dream for the one and a pleasant interlude for the other. The stranger's name was Augustus, and since they were very soon on first name terms, his surname, pronounced fleetingly only once, was soon forgotten.

When she asked where he was from, he answered, "I'm living with my uncle and guardian some miles from here. I rode here today, hardly knowing where I was going, just to get away from his constant oppression. I'm an orphan. My dear parents succumbed to a fever. Unfortunately, my father's will was written in such a way it gives my uncle control of my fortune. He's a monster, concerned with nothing but his own comfort and will permit me nothing. My only wish is to be a poet but he refuses to allow me the minimum to live on. He says I must prove myself a man by going into the army."

Like all good lies, this one was based upon the truth. Augustus Protheroe was an orphan. That is to say, his parents had died within the last five years, withered away to nothing, some said, by the knowledge that their only son was a waster and a cheat. He was now 25 years old, and in control of what was left of his fortune. He had frittered away most of it on women, gambling, and horses. He did have an uncle and was presently staying with him. He had retired to a tiny hamlet nearby and was kind enough to receive Augustus when he needed to live cheaply for a while.

His desire to be a poet was a complete invention, made up on the spot when he saw how Héloise's eyes glowed at the idea. It was true he might have to go into the army, but that was because his creditors were so hounding him, he saw no other option. Anyway, like many, he considered the August accord between the British and the French on the Iberian Peninsula would likely be of short duration. It was bound to break down and there would soon be opportunities in the army for a man like him.

He had been blessed with a handsome face and fine physique, but anyone with a little more experience would have noticed that because of his excesses, his complexion was becoming a little raddled and his waist was beginning to thicken. For him, this country maid was a honey-fall. She would serve to amuse him for a few weeks while he was forced to remain in this damned hole.

For Héloise, he was a miracle, the embodiment of all that was noble and good. He treated her with exquisite deference, touching no more than the tips of her fingers as he opened gates to allow her to pass into the newly harvested fields, or lifted the boughs of fruit-laden branches for her to pass underneath into the dappled shade. He commented with immense sensibility upon the scenes that met their eyes, from the sun sparkling on the waves down by the shore, to the glorious colors of the autumn trees edging the country lanes.

If his comments bordered on the banal, Héloise did not notice it. She was soon so intoxicated with love that anything he uttered sounded like poetry. Fingertip-touching progressed to hand holding, hand-holding to an arm around the waist, an arm around the waist to lips pressed fervently against hers, but she heard only his outpourings about love. They would live in a garret, sublimely happy, noble in their poverty, together in eternal fidelity.

It was inevitable she should ultimately surrender her body to him. In her innocence, she did not know what was happening. He certainly did and calmed her frightened protests effectively by kissing her so hard on the mouth she could hardly breathe. After the first time, she went home and into her bedchamber in a daze. It was only the disordered and stained condition of her undergarments and the pain between her legs that convinced her it had not been a dream. When she tried to explain the next day that she would prefer they not do that again, he became distraught and cried she didn't love him anymore. She gave in.

But having achieved his goal and finding after a couple of weeks that this frightened country girl was, in the end, a bit of a bore, the lover's attentions became less assiduous. Their trysts became more sporadic. He was busy, he said. He had affairs to attend to, he said. He wouldn't be able to come for a few days, he said. In the end, she waited for him one whole afternoon, then the next, and he did not come.

Chapter Eighteen

Hastings 1808-1809

Where were her protectors while this was going on? The autumn was always their busiest time, of course. Claire had gathered her hyssop and was making her distillation. Bernard and Joseph were making cider and beginning the lengthy process of Calvados production. Agnès was always busy. The treaty between France and Britain in respect of Spain meant that visitors to the continent were beginning to come down to Dover again. The peace probably wouldn't last long and those who wanted to take advantage of Paris fashions were eager to do so while they could. The inn was quite well known by now and people stopped for a meal, or overnight, sure of clean rooms and aired sheets. Alice, the vicar's wife, might have noticed Héloise's absence if she had been there, but she had gone to visit her own family at the end of the summer. The vicar, immured in his study, saw nothing. By then, Héloise was no longer having classes with him.

So the girl was left to her own sorrow. She wept bitterly for her lost love, spending days wandering to the places they had walked together, torturing herself with the memory of his soft words and tender looks. Then she began to feel unwell, especially in the mornings. Her breasts became tender and she was tired all the time. She thought this was because her heart had been truly broken, and she might die. The idea of dying of a broken heart was one Héloise was very familiar with and had no reason to disbelieve now.

Agnès was first to have suspicions when Héloise started to have to run quickly to the privy every morning. She followed the girl at a distance and heard her retching. She remembered how Claire had been. It was all familiar. She finally took Claire to one side.

"Madame, has our dear Héloise talked to you at all about... anything?"

Claire was surprised. "No, what do you mean? What should she talk about?"

"I don't want to speak out of turn, and the devil take my tongue if I'm wrong, Madame, but I think... I think she may be... increasing."

"Increasing? What can you mean? She's just a girl! She knows nothing of...."

But then she thought how her daughter's appetite had all but disappeared, how she had hollows under her eyes and was spending nearly all day in her room. She ran upstairs to the little back bedroom and there found Héloise face down on her bed, crying as if her heart would break. Claire gathered her into her arms and gradually the whole story came out.

"I thought he loved me, Maman," sobbed the girl. "But he hasn't been to see me for nearly a month! Oh, Maman, I didn't know what was happening! He said it was because he loved me. I didn't like it but... Maman, I feel so sick all the time! Is it my heart? Is it broken? Am I dying?"

A fist clutched Claire's own heart and tears came to her eyes as she realized what she should have told her daughter before. She had wanted to keep her a child, had thought there was plenty of time for all those explanations. But she had grown up so fast! She'd been so busy with her own affairs, she'd utterly failed to protect her daughter.

"Chérie," she said at last, trying not to cry herself, "No, you are not dying. And your heart cannot really break, no matter how much it may feel like it. I think the truth, my love, is that you are with child. Agnès recognized the signs. You are exactly as I was with you."

Héloise lifted her head, her tears suspended, and stared at her mother. "With child? But, it's impossible! You have to be married to have a baby!"

"No, chérie. You just have to… be with a man as you were with… oh, God, I don't even know his name!"

"Augustus. His name is Augustus. He's a poet."

"Augustus what? Who are his people?"

"I don't know! Maman! I don't know! He has an uncle… somewhere. Can we find him? If he knows I'm carrying his child, he'll marry me, won't he?" Her face was suddenly suffused with joy.

"I'll have to talk to your father about what to do." Claire thought that if this Augustus, whoever he was, had never mentioned his name, had taken advantage of her daughter and had then left without a word, he was unlikely to want to be found. Even if they could find him, would they want such a man to marry their daughter?

This was exactly Bernard's reaction when he was told the dreadful news. At first he broke down and sobbed for the lost innocence of his beloved Héloise. Then he declared he never wanted to see the man. He would never allow such a one to marry his daughter. But when Héloise threw herself at his feet and begged him to try to find Augustus, for she loved him so, he gave in. He and Joseph spent days they could ill afford riding up and down searching in vain for a person whose family name they did not know, who had been staying with an uncle no one could identify. It was probably just as well he remained undiscovered. Joseph had told Agnès he would kill him.

"Oh, Maman, what can I do?" sobbed Héloise when she realized Augustus was nowhere to be found. "I don't want to have a baby without a husband! Oh, what can I do?"

"You can do nothing, chérie. You let that baby grow inside you. You eat properly, you rest properly and most of all, you try to be glad. A baby will bring its own love, you'll see."

"But I can't be a mother! I don't know how!"

"You will learn. You'll see, it will come naturally. And Agnès and I will help you."

"But what will people say when they find I have no husband?"

"It doesn't matter what people say. We have always been and will always be foreigners here. They will say we are just like all French people and have no morals. They think that anyway, so what difference can it make?"

It was true. While now it was less frequent than at first, and although the locals enjoyed the custom attracted by the inn and were glad to sell Claire and Agnès whatever they needed, whenever there had been a dispute at the inn, they had been accused of being *bloody foreigners.* It was usually one or other of the customers drinking too much of their good home-brew and being ejected by Joseph, but they had been accused of everything, from thievery in short-changing the customers, to putting French muck in their food. Joseph would want to put them right with his fists, but Bernard always said to ignore it.

"What's the point," he said, "of sinking to their level? They already think the worst of us; we don't need to think the worst of ourselves."

Now, Héloise was seen even less frequently in the village, and almost never at the inn, where her mother kept her way from the saloon even more than before. The vicar and Alice were taken into their confidence and although they were both shocked, neither turned their back on the girl. Claire went through her old maternity clothes, put away in trunks years before, and she and Héloise spent hours refurbishing them. Héloise was one of those lucky women whose pregnancy is only visible from the front. The baby grew like a round ball in her midsection, but she expanded nowhere else. It was not until the late spring of the following year that her condition became noticeable. After her initial sickness, she felt very well.

Her son was born on the 10th of June 1809. The kindly vicar led Héloise through the traditional churching ceremony. He would have willingly foregone the confession of fault usually required at the churching of an unwed mother, but she had by now understood the true nature of her involvement with Augustus. She said her own romantic folly had been almost as much to blame as his cupidity. So she quietly confessed in the presence of her parents, Joseph, Agnès, Alice and the vicar.

When the baby was baptized, she called him Emile. She said that apart from those present at the christening, Rousseau was the only man whose words she would ever trust again.

Chapter Nineteen

Hastings 1808

After he left Héloise that last time, Augustus rode back happily to his uncle's house in Brede, an ancient village about eight miles north east of Hastings. He was satisfied with himself. That little beauty had fallen into his hands like a ripe plum. And she was a cut above the other young women he'd dallied with over the years there in the wilds of Kent. They had been a little more home-spun, so to speak. She had been, yes, he had to admit it, a young lady. Lord, how she could carry on about poetry! Quoted stuff in French and Latin, too! She'd said something about having lessons from her father and the local vicar.

How a landlady's daughter had been raised learning tripe like that he would never know. Luckily, he had retained a smattering of what he'd learned at school. Enough to fool her, anyway. Any time she said something he didn't understand, he'd just sigh and shake his head as if bowed down by the weight of the world. She would immediately ask what was wrong, and he could launch into his litany of wrongs. That would bring tears to her eyes, and provide him an opportunity to hold her closer. A little closer every time, until—well, the ripe plum was a perfect comparison.

Augustus's uncle Rupert Broadsmith was a retired civil servant, a bachelor who had filled his empty life with a love of good food and wine and British history. In London he had haunted the British Museum and dined at his own table, which he declared was the best in London. He paid his excellent cook a very handsome wage and stocked his cellar with nothing but the best.

When he retired, he had come to the village of Brede, bringing Munter, his cook, and the contents of his cellar with him. Munter was a spare, thin-faced individual who looked anything but the genius in the kitchen he was. Apart from him, Rupert Broadsmith had only a housekeeper who employed a girl from the village, and a boy to look after the one horse and the gig he kept in the stable.

"Why should I pay a valet or a butler?" he said. "I can put on my own coat and open my own damned door!"

Other than his nephew, more or less his only visitor was Squire Collingswood from next door, or at least, from the property adjacent to his. Whereas Rupert was interested in the antiquity of the area and of his house, Collingswood was interested in the land and particularly the game that resided there. Rupert quite enjoyed the shooting. That is to say, he enjoyed the products of the shoot. But he didn't care for the foxhunt. Couldn't see the point, he said. You can't eat a fox.

But Collingswood loved all forms of hunting and hosted parties during the season. He carefully tended his coverts and was proud of his reputation of providing the best sport in the area. His one nemesis was the poachers, who were as keen on his stock as he was. He never tired of complaining about them to his friend, just as his friend never tired of talking about the history of the house and village he had adopted as his own.

The village dated from Anglo-Saxon times. The first official use of its name was in a Charter from the eleventh century, but Rupert's prize possession was a much older penny with the word Brid upon it. This was believed to be the original name of the village and the penny reputed to be from way before the 1066 Norman Conquest. Over the years, both Collingswood and Augustus had been forced to listen to this repeatedly and to admire the coin every time Rupert extracted it from the special case in which it lay. While the squire paid as little attention to his friend's preoccupation as his friend did to his, Augustus quickly got to the point where he thought he should go mad if he had to hear about it one more time.

The old house Rupert had purchased was said to be Elizabethan, and he loved to draw attention to the ER cunningly carved into the ceiling timbers and the wainscoting. It was certainly drafty enough to be that old, and Augustus was careful not to visit in the colder months. But it was cool in the summer and when the evenings began to draw in, good fires in the huge hearths were very pleasant, especially after a slap-up meal with a good brandy in one's fist.

Yes, the old duffer did one very well, if one could put up with the penny business, and Augustus was glad to go there on a repairing lease from time to time. But now he had been there all of August and early September. He decided to return to London. He wanted to have one more try at a rich wife, and he was hoping the salons and ballrooms of the capital might furnish one. His finances were in a state from which he had otherwise no chance of escape, other than joining the army. A woman would be more comfortable.

He had been disappointed in the last season when the new crop of debutantes had seemingly provided him with rich fodder.

His eye had fallen upon a young heiress, said to be worth eighty thousand, and very handsome besides. He'd ordered a new wardrobe, adding to his already significant and unpaid tailor's bill, and dazzled her with his sartorial elegance and undoubted ability on the dancefloor. She fluttered her eyelashes at him, blushed over his fulsome compliments and showed every pleasure in his company.

Imagine his chagrin, when, after nearly two months of this, and just at the point he was thinking of declaring himself, her engagement was announced to the scion of an old and wealthy family. He was stunned. Where had this come from? She had positively encouraged his advances. He had thought himself home and dry.

It turned out this engagement was a long-standing pre-arranged affair between the families. All the while he had thought he was dazzling the heiress, she had been misleading him with her coy glances and shy blushes. A fixed smile on his face, he gently reproached her one evening soon after the announcement had been made.

"I thought you loved me, my dear," he said, taking her hand.

"Oh, I do!" she replied. "You have been wonderful! I begged Mama and Papa to allow me one season before getting engaged, and I'm so glad I did! It's been the most tremendous fun, hasn't it?" Then, seeing the disgruntled look that, despite his sincere attempts to prevent it, appeared upon his face, "But surely you knew I was promised to Casper? I thought everyone did!"

"No, I didn't. You should have told me."

"But you can't possibly have thought my Papa would have favored a suit by you? I'm told you haven't two pennies to rub together!" She laughed gaily. "But you are the most wonderful dancer!"

He never spoke to her again.

Chapter Twenty

London 1808

Now, coming back to London after two months rusticating, Augustus found the heiress already married and on a protracted trip to the Continent. A number of the other equally well-favored though rather less wealthy damsels he had previously ignored were now betrothed to other men. The pickings were distinctly slim. His case was getting desperate. He had borrowed to pay for his new wardrobe back in the spring and both the cent-per-cent merchant and his tailor, whose astronomically high bill had only partially been satisfied, were now dunning him. With the image of the Army growing ever more insistent, he needed an advantageous marriage, or the promise of one.

The only possibility left to him was Mildred Waterbury, a not ill-favored young woman, whose visage was nonetheless marred by a permanent expression of ill-temper. She had been hanging out for a husband the last two seasons. She held men in poor regard in general, and was only prepared to look for a mate to enable her to assume control of her own fortune and escape the confines of a home ruled over by her equally ill-tempered mother. The *on-dit* was that Lady Waterbury had driven the meek Lord Waterbury to an early grave by her constant nagging and criticism. Mildred appeared to share these qualities with her mother and as a consequence had not been besieged by would-be suitors during either of her seasons.

Augustus now realized he had little choice. He convinced himself that once the first flush of their union was passed, he would be able to deal with an ill-tempered wife by the simple expedient of ignoring her altogether. It was well known that in many of the upper-class families husband and wife led entirely separate lives. He would be happy with that. Accordingly he began to pay her court, smiled when she made cutting comments about others and forced a look of polite acquiescence onto his face when she made only slightly less disparaging remarks about himself.

"Caper-merchant!" she said nastily on one occasion when he had returned to her after dancing with another lady, for she herself did not dance.

"As you say, as you say, my dear Miss Waterbury," he replied. "One's humble best is bound not to find approval by such a fine judge as you."

"'Pon my word, Mr. Protheroe," she exclaimed, (for such was the family name Héloise had failed to register) "you are mighty complaisant when one gives you a set-down."

"When it comes from one whose judgement one admires," he replied with a bow, "one is forced to accept the justice of it. Whatever you accuse me of I'm sure I deserve."

"Hmph!" came the response. Miss Waterbury, unlike Héloise, clearly saw the signs of dissipation writ upon his person, but thought he was probably the best she was likely to get.

The courtship progressed, if that is the word, with the gentleman pressing and the lady seemingly untouched by his blandishments, until at the end of October Augustus felt he might try his luck. He sent a note to the rather gloomy Waterbury townhouse that he would be honored if Miss Waterbury would receive him at 11 o'clock the following morning.

With unusual self-denial, he was home only shortly after midnight the evening before and went early to bed, so that he might have sufficient time to prepare himself the next day. Mornings were not his best time. He did not generally arise before noon, and then with bloodshot eyes and a yellowish cast to his countenance, evidence of the travails of his poor liver to process the quantity of alcohol he generally consumed. But even after an abstemious evening and early night, it took him an hour and several cups of coffee before he could consider getting up and dressed.

This last was a challenge these days, since Skipton, his valet, was careless in his attentions. He had not been paid in six months and was actively seeking a new position. His sister had recently been taken on as dresser to Lady Pevensey, when her old one was pensioned off. Unfortunately, there was no post for Skipton in that household, Lord Pevensey having died in some sort of accident.

Now, when his master called for the yellow waistcoat, he brought the blue one. Augustus cursed him and sent him to find what he had asked for. Then his best coat, that should have been properly attended to before being put away the last time it was worn, was discovered to have wine stains. With another oath, Augustus had to begin again, calling back the discarded blue waistcoat to go with his second-best coat.

Finally dressed, he surveyed himself. He had never been altogether satisfied with the fit of this coat. It wasn't quite sufficiently cut into the waist and the shoulders sloped a trifle, but knowing how much he still owed his tailor, he had not dared to ask for alterations and had instead ordered another. But there was nothing he could do about it now. As it was, he was barely ready in time to take his phaeton, a high-perch he still hadn't paid for, to the old-fashioned but good Waterbury address.

He was shown into the tall townhouse by a somber butler, who led him to the salon and told him to wait. As he waited, for Mildred certainly did not hurry, he looked around. The tall windows were heavily draped and very little light shone in. This was to his advantage, as the effects of his dissipation were less visible on his face. But it made it difficult to see clearly and the heavy William and Mary furniture, deeply carved and no doubt considered beautiful a generation ago, squatted squarely in the gloom. Dark oil paintings hung on walls papered in a color that might once have been yellow, but was now an indeterminate shade of dirty beige.

Nonetheless he surveyed it all with some appreciation. He saw careful husbanding of old money. The furniture had not been replaced with the more popular Queen Anne style found in most London townhomes. The dark portraits, of which the subjects were impossible to discern, were probably those of ancestors, another testimony to the age of the family. Yes, he could deal with that. Old money, new money. It was all the same to him, so long as he could spend it.

Mildred at length appeared, her stately carriage excellent as always. She entered the room, but did not hold out her hand in anything like friendship. Neither did she sit.

Augustus stood and bowed and then felt somewhat uncomfortable. Should he launch right into it or make small talk for a while? In the event, matters were taken out of his hands. He should have seen the signs of how things were to be, but he didn't and was to live to regret it.

"Mr. Protheroe," she said. "I believe you have something to say to me?"

"Er... yes," stammered her suitor, his ready address deserting him in his hour of real need. "I... er... I...."

"Yes, well, get on with it," snapped his beloved. "You want to marry me, is that it?"

"Er... since you mention it, er... yes, that's it exactly," said Augustus, recovering a little. He hesitated then went down on one knee.

"Dear Miss Waterbury," he began. She gave him no sign of encouragement. "Will you do me the honor... er, the great honor, of accepting my name and my hand in marriage?"

She backed away and began walking slowly up and down, leaving him stranded there, wondering whether he should rise or stay where he was.

"Will I accept your name and hand?" she said, as if thinking out loud. "Well, I need to get married to assume control of my fortune and the estate. I suppose you're the best I'm likely to get at this point." She was silent for a moment. Then, "You're not bad looking and you've good manners, so that's something. On the other hand, you're done up, living on tick, and will need me to pay your bills, so you're bound to cost me a good deal of the ready."

Augustus was so shocked to hear the unladylike vocabulary issuing from his beloved's mouth that he forgot to be shocked she knew all about his debts.

She turned back to him. "Get up, for heaven's sake," she snapped. "You look an idiot kneeling there like that." She paused. "Very well, then. I could do worse and as I said, I'm not likely to do better. I don't want to be the unmarried daughter living at home with her mother, so I accept."

Rising thankfully to his feet, Augustus responded conventionally, if not altogether truthfully, "Then you make me the happiest of men."

"I doubt it," replied Mildred coldly, "but I will pay your debts."

"My dear," said her betrothed, taking her hand, "I'm sure I will go over all that with your man of business. No need to bother your head about it all."

"Hmph!" said Mildred, deciding not to inform him it was she who would decide "all that". Her man of business, a meek fellow not unlike her late father, would do exactly as she told him.

It would be an exaggeration to say that Augustus was a happy man as he drove back to his lodgings in his high-perch phaeton, but he was experiencing a degree of relief. Once they knew he was betrothed to an heiress, the tradespeople would cease dunning him. In fact, he reflected, it might be a good idea to order a few new necessities now in case things were more difficult later. He suddenly remembered her announcement "I shall pay your bills" and had the uncomfortable thought that his betrothed might not leave the financial affairs of the family entirely in his hands, as he had supposed.

Still, he consoled himself, she obviously didn't want a husband with debts all over town. He thought he would be able to use that intelligence to his advantage in the future.

Chapter Twenty-One

Berkshire 1809

Three months later, Augustus knew better. His first shock had been his interview with the family man of business, the meek Mr. Colby. It had been far from satisfactory.

"Good afternoon, Colby," he had begun in a bluff man-to-man tone. "Let's see what we can work out between us."

"I'm afraid, sir," the man had replied, "there isn't much for us to work out. His late lordship's will specifically states that Miss Waterbury is to assume full personal control of her fortune and the Waterbury estate when she marries. The expenses of Lady Waterbury's London residence are to be met from the estate, but she will live on her own fortune. My job will be to follow both ladies' directions."

He did not say that it was he who had drawn up the will in the presence of his lordship and his wife and daughter, and there had been no doubt as to who had been in charge. It was not Lord Waterbury.

Augustus let that sink in. Then he asked, with misgivings, "Has she said anything about my... er, settlement?"

"No, sir. She has directed me to pay your debts, however. To that end, I would be obliged if you would send me a list."

"So you've no inkling what I might have to... to play with, so to speak?"

"No idea whatsoever, sir, I'm sorry. You will have to speak to Miss Waterbury."

Mr. Colby might be meek, but mentally he was not mild. He had not formed a very good impression of Mr. Protheroe. *All mouth and trousers* was what, in one of his frequent interior dialogs, he said to himself. He might have told the future husband of his client that in his opinion, formed of many years dealing with the Waterbury women, he was unlikely to get very much out of his future spouse. *Cold as a nun's tit* was the expression he used in his head, but of course, did not utter.

Augustus left the interview rather shaken. He had never envisaged that he would have to apply to his wife for funds. He had assumed this would all be dealt with man-to-man. His first thought was whether he could somehow get out of his betrothal. But two things militated against it. First, he would be considered a poltroon and a cad if he withdrew. No other woman of the *ton*, much less an heiress, would ever look at him. Secondly, he had also already ordered more clothes from his tailor, boots from Hoby's and other trifles including a new hat, gloves, and a fine cane with a heavy gold ferrule. He would never have the means to pay for any of it, not to mention his earlier debts, if he did not marry Mildred. He sighed. Then his natural buoyancy reasserted itself. He would damned well make sure his wife loved him to distraction and would give him whatever he wanted. He was a fine figure of a man, he knew how to love a woman. After the wedding night, she would be wax in his hands.

His next great shock came after the wedding ceremony. It had never occurred to Augustus that they would not stay at least half the year in London. He had failed to understand the implication of Mr. Colby's words about the expenses of Lady Waterbury's London residence. He had even begun to make plans as to which of the rooms he would adopt as his own. He rather thought the library. Not that he planned to do any reading, but no one ever went in there; he would be safe from the two unpleasant women in the house.

And then he had, of course, thought they would take a wedding trip. Images of pleasant *taverna* in Greece filled his mind. In vain had he argued that it was the time of year when a trip to the Aegean would be pleasant. Besides, he wished to introduce his wife to the beauties of the ancient world. But Mildred had never been abroad and had no intention of doing so. She considered all foreigners inferior, and had no estimation at all of anything they or their forebears might have produced. She was absolutely opposed to a trip of any sort. They would stay at home. By that, Augustus assumed they meant London.

They married early in the morning on a cold day in January and it was as they were descending the steps at St. George's Chapel that he fully appreciated the nature of the life he had chosen for himself.

"Well, my dear," he said to his new wife. "You rightly chose not to waste money on a wedding breakfast for people we hardly know, so where shall we go for the bang-up meal to celebrate our nuptials? With your dear mama, of course."

He had thought he was doing well to leave her to decide on where their private celebration should be, but her response staggered him.

"We shall go nowhere. We return to Waterbury House to pick up our luggage then leave immediately for Berkshire. I wish to arrive before nightfall. We will have a light nuncheon when we change the horses."

"You mean we are not to stay in London at all?"

"No, of course not. Waterbury House is to be Mama's exclusively. Did Mr. Colby not make that clear? We shall make our home in the country. There is much to do, and now I am mistress of the estate, I intend to do it."

In fact, Lady Waterbury had no wish to entertain her daughter and son-in-law. She was glad to have Mildred off her hands. Though they both had a very poor opinion of men and had been united in bullying the poor late peer, they had never particularly liked each other.

So Mr. and Mrs. Protheroe, or Lady Mildred, as she preferred to be called, settled into life in a large, inconvenient, and damp house near Reading. Or, at least, one of them settled in with a will, and the other was reluctantly forced to do so. Its lands were bordered on one side by the River Tennant and grew wheat and barley, both used in the local brewing industry.

The late Lord Waterbury had been well known for escaping into the town to taste the local beer, for which it was famous. In fact, it was through an accident after an evening of more than usually heavy imbibing that he met his end. He had caused his carriage to stop and let him down so that he might relieve himself into the river. He had lost his footing and fallen into the water. Since he, too, had drunk rather more than was good for him, his coachman did not hear his cries, and by the time he began to wonder where his lordship had got to, the unfortunate peer's body had been washed away. It was found a day or so later in a downstream eddy. Since this happened a few days after the writing of the Will, which may, indeed, have been the cause of his lordship's over-imbibing in the first place, his wife and daughter were not unduly sorrowful.

"He always was an idiot," was his wife's fond epitaph.

Chapter Twenty-Two

Berkshire 1809

On their wedding night, when Augustus tried to consummate the marriage, Mildred waved him away.

"I'm too tired for any of that nonsense tonight," she said. "It's been a long day and I need my sleep. You may try tomorrow."

"But, my dear," he protested. "It's the culmination of the day. The most important part, you might almost say."

"You might, but I certainly wouldn't," she retorted. "From what Mama told me it seems an unpleasant and messy experience. I'm quite happy to put it off."

"I said NO!" she protested loudly when he tried to take her in his arms. "Go to your room!"

He felt like nothing so much as a chastised schoolboy, but in the end did as she said. He crept away to his large, drafty chamber, with bed hangings and curtains that looked as if they might not have been refurbished in over fifty years, and furniture that most certainly had not. There was no brick in bed. Presumably the maids thought he would not be sleeping there. He didn't like to ring and give them all something to gossip about, so lay there in the frigid sheets—probably not aired—until he fell asleep.

It has already been noted that Augustus was not an early riser. The following morning he was, however, awoken by a peremptory knock at his door and opened a bleary eye to see his wife sailing in and, although it was only just gone eight, already dressed and apparently ready to greet the world.

"Get up," she said. "There will be no lazing around now I'm lady of the estate. Today we must begin a visit of the tenants, let them get a look at you so they won't shoot you for a poacher the first time you ride out across the fields." She laughed heartily at her own joke and turned to leave. "Breakfast won't be served later than nine o'clock. We keep country hours here. If you want something to eat, you'd better shake a leg." She left.

Not for the first time, Augustus wondered at the low tone of her ladyship's speech. *Shake a leg*, indeed! He lay there for a while wondering if he had not made the biggest mistake of his life, and thinking it would have been better to tell his creditors to go to hell. They couldn't get blood out of a stone. In the end, because he needed a cup of coffee more than anything else, he rang for Skipton and prepared to meet the day.

He felt slightly better as all the servants he saw on the way downstairs curtseyed or bowed and the stately butler led him with some ceremony to the dining room. His wife was seated at one end of an enormously long table, already immersed in a pile of papers. She looked up briefly as he entered.

"You're here at last," she said, with no warmth in her tone. "Take your place and order what you want."

It turned out that his place was at the other end of the table, so that it was almost impossible to engage in conversation unless one was prepared to shout. He was not. He asked for coffee and then said to the butler, "Before you go, won't you ask her ladyship if we might sit a little closer together? Perhaps some leaves might be taken out of the table?"

The butler made his stately way down to the other end and Augustus saw him lean towards Mildred and gesture towards him. He received some sort of reply and walked slowly back to Augustus.

"Her ladyship says she sees no reason for you to be closer. The table has always been like this since before her grandfather's time and it will not now be changed. I shall bring your coffee directly, sir. Are you sure you desire nothing else?"

"No." Augustus waved him away. "I rarely eat breakfast." He did not add that he was usually not out of his bed at what might be considered breakfast time.

A footman brought in a plate of something and placed it in front of Mildred, who paid him no attention whatsoever. Augustus was too far away to see what was on her plate, but his wife evidently enjoyed it, shoveling it into her mouth with little finesse.

The butler returned with a pot of coffee and one cup, poured it out and was about to place the pot on the table at Augustus's elbow when Mildred caught sight of it and shouted from the other end of the table, "Is that coffee? Bring it here."

The pot was transported to the other end of the table, a cup was refilled and Mildred said, "Leave the pot here. I might want some more."

That was the last Augustus saw of his coffee. He was damned if he was going to walk down there and get it.

Chapter Twenty-Three

Berkshire 1809

And so it went on. His new bride showed Augustus no love or even friendship. She ordered him hither and thither and if he showed any hesitation, hectored him like a school mistress. She refused to allow him near her until five days later when she announced in her commanding tone at the end of dinner, oblivious to the fact that the butler was still in the room, "You may visit me tonight. I shall be waiting."

By this time, Augustus's dream of bringing her to heel by his expertise as a lover had completely evaporated. In fact, he had lost all desire to validate the marriage in the usual way. He was afraid he might not even be able to do it, so intense was his dislike of his bride by now. He wondered whether he might still be able to put an end to the whole thing by claiming non-consummation.

In the event, when he presented himself to her later that night, she had blown out all the candles and for one hopeful moment he thought she might be asleep.

But no, her voice came sharply out of the gloom, "Well, get on with it, I haven't got all night."

He was actually grateful for the dark, because he could in the end perform the task by imagining he was with someone else.

What was the name of that little piece he'd had down in Hastings? Eleanor? No... Eloise. That was it. Eloise.

If he thought his exertions in the bedroom might soften his wife's heart, he was mistaken. There was no pillow talk. She dismissed him immediately afterwards and he went back to his own room feeling like a workaday bull that had serviced a prize heifer. He tried on one or two occasions to find out what sort of settlement she had planned for him, for although his bills had been paid, there had been no mention of an allowance. Finally, he went boldly into the office where she spent most mornings, poring over huge piles of records from the estate, and asked to speak to her. He felt like a supplicant asking for a Papal audience.

"You always seem so busy, my dear," he said humbly, "I wish you would let me help you!"

"You, help me?" she replied scornfully, "A man who could not even keep his own miserable affairs in order, help me with the running of a large estate? I think not. In fact, it is because of the poor management already exercised by two other men—my father and the manager—that I find us in a parlous state. Steps will have to be taken."

"Oh. I see. But," he said desperately, "do you have a minute to talk to me about my... my allowance?"

He hated to use that word. It made him sound like a schoolboy.

"What do you mean, *allowance*?" she returned, looking narrowly at him.

"Well, you know... er... personal expenses, clothes, that sort of thing."

"I can't imagine what personal expenses you can have, Augustus. Everything you need is paid for, and as for clothes, I should think, by going over your bills before we were married, that you have enough to last you a lifetime."

"You saw my bills?" he gulped.

"Certainly, you don't think Colby would have paid them without my permission, do you?"

"No," he replied miserably.

"In fact," she continued, as if he had not spoken. "I paid for that ridiculous high-perch phaeton of yours, I don't know why, because now we're living in the country, you will have no need of it. I've instructed Colby to sell it and put the horses up at Tattersall's."

"But," he almost shouted, "I just sent him word to have it brought here! I thought to use it!"

"Ridiculous! Such a thing on country lanes! You would be overturned in a moment!"

"I'll have you know," he began, half rising from his seat, "I'm thought to be a considerable whip!"

"That's as may be, but it won't do you any good here. Anyway, it will be sold, as I directed. If you need to ride out, you may use the gig."

"The gig!" he exclaimed. You cannot expect me to appear in a gig!"

"As you wish. If you do not care for the gig, though it suited my father perfectly well, you may saddle one of the horses when you go around on estate business."

"Estate business? What estate business?"

"I have decided to get rid of the ineffective manager we currently employ and put you in his place."

"I know nothing about running an estate."

"Of course you don't. But you will not need to know anything. You will simply follow my instructions. You will report to me here every morning at nine and I shall give you a list of things to do. You may take a groom to show you the way at first, but after a while you will dispense with the groom. I do not wish to employ two people to do one man's job."

"Employing… job…," he stuttered. "Dammit all, Mildred, I'm your husband, not an employee!"

"If," she continued as if she had not heard him, "if you perform the work satisfactorily, I shall pay you a wage. Not as much as I currently pay the manager, since you are already housed and fed at the expense of the estate, but it will provide you with something of an… allowance, as you called it. We shall begin tomorrow morning at nine sharp. Don't be late."

Augustus stumbled away from this audience in horror. He racked his brains for a way out. But where was he to go? And how was he to get there? He had not a penny piece in his pocket. He knew at last he had met his match. All the wiles and subtleties he had used with both men and women all his life were useless to him now. He was fixed, like a butterfly on a pin.

In the following months, the timetable he was forced to follow weighed on him dreadfully. He had been accustomed to staying in the country with friends or even his uncle. But there, though dinner was taken early, the evenings afterwards were enlivened by a hand of whist, a game of billiards, or, in the case of friends, a mild flirtation, or perhaps even more, with one or other of the women in the party.

Here, dinner was taken at seven and was over by eight. Mildred took herself off to her own chambers and he was left to his own devices. He had no money and nowhere to go, so he would have a brandy or two on his own by the fire in the salon. On the first occasion he tried to order more, the butler told him her ladyship had given him orders to serve no more than two, and the bottle was kept, along with all the others, under lock and key. He tried the billiard room, but the baize was in such poor condition it was impossible to play. He wound up retiring to his own room at the incredible hour of ten and spending the next couple of hours staring disconsolately at the ceiling.

He was entirely unaccustomed to such a timetable, and found he would fall into a disturbed sleep, wake up between two and three in the morning then fall asleep again at about five. Left to his own devices he might then sleep till nine or ten, but that luxury was not to be allowed him.

The morning after Mildred's disclosure of what was to be his function at the estate, his man woke him at seven with coffee. He drank two cups on a very empty stomach, not having eaten anything since seven the night before, and began the lengthy procedure of getting dressed. He told himself he was not going to let his standards of personal attire drop, no matter what, so that first day he appeared before her looking the positive picture of the wealthy man about town, from his faultless jacket to his polished top boots. The top boots were, indeed, the only concession he made to country life. He could not ride in his Hessians. He would wear his many-caped topcoat and curly beaver, and he carried his walking stick with the gold ferrule under his arm.

"If you think that's a suitable rig-out for visiting tenant farms and wading through mud to collect back rent, I think you'll find yourself disappointed. But no matter, you'll learn," said his wife, eying him up and down. "Now these are the farms you will visit today. Next to each is the sum owed in rent. You will collect it and bring it back. If the farmer claims he is unable to pay, you will tell him he has till next quarter to come up with it or he and his family will be put out. You will accept no excuses. Is that understood? Peter the groom will accompany you for a couple of weeks until you learn the lie of the land. That will be all."

Augustus dumbly took the sheaf of papers she handed him and walked slowly to the stables.

Chapter Twenty-Four

Hastings 1809-1814

Motherhood was a joy to Héloise, young as she was. As Claire had said, the baby brought his own love. He was a smiling infant who grew into a happy child, not surprisingly, since he had five adults to wait on him hand, foot, and finger. They made no explanation to the people in the village as to who his father was. When an inn customer once suggested it was Joseph, he picked him up by the scruff of the neck and threw him physically out of the door, telling him never to return. In spite of protestations it was all a joke, the customer was never again allowed on the premises. The others learned the lesson. In fact, no one was surprised the young woman should have succumbed to the temptations of the flesh. It was common enough.

Emile was educated much as Héloise herself had been. Both French and English were spoken routinely in the household. Agnès sang him the same songs in the kitchen she used to sing to his mother, and Héloise told him the same stories her mother had told her. When he was old enough to begin formal instruction, the Vicar's wife, delighted to have another child in the vicarage, undertook elementary English. Héloise herself taught him to read and write in French.

He was not quite the student his mother had been, and as soon as he could he would be outside, running with the village children and learning the broadest Sussex dialect. Claire at first protested that he should be kept apart, as Héloise had been. But his mother remembered how lonely she had been once the vicarage twins had left for Eton, and now realized that if she had had a few girls of her own age to talk to, she might not have been such an easy prey for Augustus. She decided to let Emile be a child amongst children.

The boy seemed to understand instinctively where and how he should speak what. Hearing him with his cohorts in the village, one would have taken him for a farmer's lad. But when he was with his grandparents he spoke the purest French, and with Alice in the vicarage his English was complete Mayfair.

Nevertheless, Héloise worried about Emile's future. Although she now had the lowest opinion of Augustus, her son was the offspring of a gentleman, as she was herself. When her son was five, she asked advice of her old mentor, the vicar.

"I want Emile to be a gentleman," she explained to him one day. "A better one than his father, to be sure. I think I understand that the first step would be to enroll him at Eton, like Sebastian and Oliver. Do you think that's possible?"

The kindly vicar looked at her over the top of his pince-nez. "Are you sure that's what you want?" he asked.

"Yes. I've thought and thought about it and I've decided it's my responsibility to give him the means of moving up in the world. You know Maman and Papa aren't innkeepers by upbringing. It was a pure accident they ended up here. They've made a good life for themselves and for me, but if he stays here, he will have no choice but to end up working at the inn. There's nothing wrong with that, but I know if I asked them, they would feel as I do that Emile deserves to have more opportunity: the law or the church, like yourself, for example.

"You're not afraid you might lose him? Once he finds a different type of society, he may not want to return to this one."

"I've thought about that, too, and I know it's a possibility. Nonetheless, I want him to have the choice."

"Well, when the time comes," said the vicar, "I can probably use a little influence to get him accepted at Eton. All the men in my family have gone there over the years."

Héloise thanked him, kissed him on the cheek and walked slowly home, planning.

"Maman," she said to her mother when she got home, "When Emile is old enough I should like to send him to Eton, like the vicarage twins. Reverend Beresford says he can probably arrange it. Do you think there is any way we can afford it?"

Over the years, Bernard and Joseph had settled in to running the bar at the inn, perfecting the Calvados, beer, and cider production. Agnès ran the kitchen with an iron hand, nowadays with help from a village girl, who couldn't understand a word she said and had to be taught by mime and pointing, and the occasional cuff behind the ear if she didn't get it right.

Claire took care of the guest rooms and, building upon what old Madeleine had taught her all those years ago, she had also become adept at using local herbs and plants for home remedies. She had discovered some of these in the same book where her husband had found his first introduction to beer and cider production. Then one day she fell into conversation with the grandmother of a woman from whom they bought some of their supplies. As a young woman in the previous century, when there had been no doctor within miles, she had helped her own mother with country cures. It took some effort to decipher the old woman's speech, and especially the local names for plants, but at length Claire was able to learn a great deal. She was now sought out for cures of various kinds, from wrenched shoulders to earache. She also often helped local women with various aspects of pregnancy, which was both the happiness and despair of their lives.

So when Héloise asked her mother whether they would be able to afford the fees for Eton, the answer was a tentative yes. The inn was doing well enough between regular customers, Agnès's meals and the summer visitors. And though she never felt comfortable asking much from the poor country folk, Claire was earning a little with her cures. Her nest-egg was growing, pennies at a time.

Then, just as things were going well, disaster struck the little group of émigré innkeepers. The winter of 1814 was the coldest anyone could remember. In London, the Thames froze solid and a winter fair was held on its surface. Snow fell even along the south coast, where it was almost unknown. Canterbury was cut off completely for five days and a Mail coach drove off the road into a snow-covered ditch outside Maidenhead. For days, fog rolled in from the sea and made it impossible to see more than a few feet ahead. All traffic to the inn came to a halt, except for the few locals who walked through drifts to get there. Bernard, who rarely got though a winter without illness, succumbed to a serious inflammation of the lungs. Claire sat with him day and night, cupping him, depleting her store of hyssop balm, and trying one thing after another. In spite of everything she could do, on a miserable, dark day in February, he died.

The little family was devastated and Claire was inconsolable. She had adored her husband from the moment they had met, back in those summer days in Bordeaux, long ago. She blamed herself for not being able to save him. They had called in the doctor but he had been delayed by snowdrifts. Although he assured Claire there was nothing anyone could have done better, she wept under a weight of guilt. Agnès, who rarely cried, vanished into her kitchen and was later discovered by Joseph, who like many big men was very softhearted and himself had tears in his eyes, with her apron flung over her head, crying as if her heart would break.

Héloise was numb and wandered up to her room in shock until the necessity of explaining it all to Emile made her pull herself together. The loss of that gentle, scholarly man whom fate had turned into an innkeeper and who was prouder of the callouses on his hands than the flowing sentences his pen could write, was the hardest blow of her life, harder than the abandonment by a man she thought had loved her and who had left her with his child.

The émigrés had not realized how much a part of the village they had become until small gifts of bread, eggs, a pigeon, or a hare began arriving at the kitchen door. The little church was packed for the funeral service. Five men came forward unasked to help Joseph shoulder the coffin and carry it out of the church. The congregation rose as one to follow it to the small stone house where the body would be kept until the weather permitted the digging of a grave. In the spring, which came very late that year, the family returned to lay Bernard to rest, far from home but in a place he had come to love. With the vicar's help, they ordered a stone to mark the grave. Its inscription read: *Here lies Bernard Rambuteau, A Man of Liberty, Equality, Fraternity.*

Joseph took seeds from one of the apples they kept in the cellar and carefully grew them indoors in the sunniest spot he could find. In such a terrible winter that was a labor of love. When the spring finally came, he put the hardiest seedlings outside until one of them was grown and vigorous enough to provide the root stock for a graft from one of the trees whose fruit they used for Calvados. By the beginning of the summer, he was able to plant it at the foot of Bernard's grave. He would go there often, ostensibly to tend it, but in reality to confer with the man who was both master and friend.

They would have closed *The Traveller's Rest* for the rest of the winter, but Agnès said she would go mad without something to do, and Joseph said he didn't have the heart to turn away someone knocking on the door after struggling to get there. He said he could manage well enough on his own, but he was no longer a young man and when Claire saw how tired he was getting, she insisted they hire some help. One of the pallbearers, a fellow gardener, was glad of the job. The day to day running of the inn was assured, but Joseph wondered how he would be able to carry on the making of the Calvados without Bernard. The beer and cider he could manage, but Bernard had been the French liqueur expert.

Chapter Twenty-Five

Berkshire 1809-1814

The first time Augustus did his rounds as manager of the estate, he was gratified by the doffing of caps and curtsies he met wherever he went. This helped slightly to assuage his anger and despair at the position he was in, but it was a dreadful day. He delivered the messages to the tenant farmers, mostly about unpaid rent but occasionally complaints about poor fencing or clogged ditches. He tried as far as possible to stay on his horse, so as not to sully his boots or splash his jacket any more than it already was from the mud thrown up by the horse's hooves. Nevertheless, by the time he got home, hungry (for he had eaten neither breakfast nor lunch), late and tired, he was also filthy.

"I'll just have a bath, my dear," he said to his wife, who was calmly sitting by the fire in the salon.

"No you won't," she replied, lifting her head from whatever it was she was reading (probably Dante's *Inferno*, looking for tips, thought her husband), "You'll be late for dinner. Just take off your muddy things and change quickly. I said you were dressed too fine."

And she continued her perusal of the book in her hand.

He sullenly did as he was bid, cleaning up as best he could in the cold water from the jug in his room and then turned to the clothing his valet had put out for him. Skipton had been paid and was now quite enjoying life as the Master's valet which gave him precedence in the kitchen over all but the butler. His existence was a good deal more comfortable than Augustus's. The servants' table was stinted neither food nor drink, for the housekeeper, a canny woman who had been with the family for years, knew how to pad the expenses just enough to keep the below-stairs very comfortably without appearing to spend more than the bare minimum. She was the only person who had ever outdone Mildred, a fact of which she was happily aware but her mistress was not.

As he looked at the evening clothing laid out on the bed, Augustus rebelled.

"Dammit," he said, "I'm not going to all that trouble. Just bring me clean britches and a coat. I'll keep the rest on."

Skipton raised his brows, but said nothing. It suited him fine if his master didn't change properly for dinner. Less for him to take care of.

"Make sure you clean my top boots and give the cloak a good brush. And for tomorrow, look out my oldest stuff. It's no good dressing up in this god-forsaken hole."

And so it went on. His days were all like the first. The only differences were that Augustus began to rise early enough to eat a proper breakfast and he learned how to position himself to get something of a lunch. If he got off his horse and walked into the farmer's kitchen on some pretext or other at around lunchtime, he was bound to be offered a bite to eat. It might only be bread and cheese, but it kept him going.

He found the tenants a good deal better company than his wife, and, as he got to know them, would pass the time of day talking with them. They mostly discussed the weather and the crops at first, but as he got to know the younger men better, he would regale them with tales of his life in London, both real and invented. This, together with the fact that daily work and a regular diet broadened his shoulders and slimmed his stomach, gave him the reputation of a real out-and-outer. The young men admired him and the girls adored him.

Imperceptibly, without realizing it, he began to learn how to run an estate and, moreover, to enjoy it. As the winter gave way to spring and the spring to summer, for the first time in his life he appreciated the change of the seasons other than as a moment to visit his tailor and order new suits.

Mildred was as good as her word and after the first month began to pay him a salary. It wasn't much, but it afforded him a degree of freedom. As he became familiar with the place and could dispense with an accompanying groom, a good percentage of his meager wages found its way into the village innkeeper's pocket. Like Mildred's father, he soon found the home-brew very much to his taste.

Even more to his taste were the innkeeper's plump daughters who, like their mother before them, were prepared, at a modest price, to be generous to their male clients, and especially the Master. The innkeeper himself, who profited from a bit of poaching, was happy for his daughters to repay, in their way, the blind eye of the Lord of the Manor and his gamekeeper. Everyone was satisfied.

Like the housekeeper, Augustus was careful. His trysts kept him late on no more occasions than could be explained by a lost horseshoe, a flooded lane, an upturned hay wain, or simply the beauty of the summer evening that he claimed made him loiter on the way home. Thus, five years went by and Augustus forgot all about leaving.

Chapter Twenty-Six

Berkshire 1815

There was one time of year that Augustus did not enjoy at all, and that was the annual visit of Mildred's mother. That formidable dowager liked to escape the heat of London in July and August by coming to the ancestral home. She found fault with everything, which annoyed her daughter and made her, in turn, even sharper with Augustus. Really, the wood paneling in the hall needed a good polish. Anyone could see that. The place had never looked so dusty in her day! The servants had to be kept up to snuff. And the furnishings in the salon were so faded from the sun! Did no one think to close the curtains in the afternoons? And the sheets! She had positively put her foot through one on her bed! And no wonder! They were so thin one could practically read the newspaper through them! Let them be sewn sides to middle. There was plenty of wear in them that way. But don't put any sewn-up sheets on her bed, thank you! And so it went on.

Mildred harangued her husband every day about problems that were all in some way attributable to his negligence. Why was young Thompson still in arrears with his rent? And apparently the yield of barley in the top field was way down. What had he done about it? In vain did Augustus argue that Thompson's wife had been poorly after the birth of their first child and he had been unable to do all the work by himself, or that the flooding in the top field, where he had told her extra drainage was needed before they planted the barley, had caused the low yield. It was always all his fault.

It was the habit of Mildred and her mother to take a ride in the gig in the late afternoon, when the heat of the day was over. Although normally attached to the outward show of belonging to the class of society that needs to be waited on at every turn, they did not always take a groom. This was because they enjoyed discussing very freely and ridiculing everyone they knew, including the local neighbors. Consequently, whenever they had no intention of stopping anywhere or descending from the gig, they went alone. Mildred would take the reins, with her mother beside her, and as soon as they were clear of the house, they would launch into speech that would have amazed those who thought them very proper ladies.

Augustus featured frequently as their main object of scorn. The tenants preferred him to his mean-spirited wife, so kept quiet about his amorous adventures in the village. Both she and her mother considered him a very poor excuse for a man. On this occasion, it was the lack of any sign of a child that exercised the older woman's mind. Mildred and Augustus had, after all, now been married five years.

"Is he unable to perform?" she asked her daughter, with no beating about the bush. "Your father was often so limp he was no use at all."

"Well, he can usually begin all right, but he's so rapid, I sometimes wonder whether anything is produced," replied Mildred, with equal candor.

She did not say that she only permitted Augustus near her about once a month. For his part, he only went to her chamber when she directed him to do so. He deliberately made the coupling as rapid as possible, usually dwelling on the attractions of the innkeeper's daughters as he lay with his wife in the dark.

"Something must be done," said her mother firmly.

Unknown to them, something had been done. It would materially change the outlook for all concerned.

After tenderly helping them into the gig that afternoon, Augustus had gone to the front, ostensibly to check the horse's harness, and quickly slipped a prickly burr under each side of the nose band where it met the bit rein. His objective was to make the horse restive and difficult to control, so that their ride would be unpleasant. It was a mean little trick, and he laughed to himself as they set off.

Mildred was an impatient driver. She had been told, but never learned, that a soft touch is all that is needed for a well-trained horse. The horse was well-trained, the driver was not. She shook the reins constantly, and every time she did so, the burrs under the noseband pressed against the animal's cheeks. He tossed his head and waved it from side to side, which should have been a sign that something was wrong. But the two women were so engaged in their discussion of Augustus's shortcomings in the bedroom that they didn't notice.

Mildred's grandfather had bought the gig they were riding in. He firmly believed in buying the best. The metal railings on either side were of the first quality iron, and the wooden body underneath was of solid oak. However, her father had been a poor manager, and Mildred's penny-pinching disposition caused her to ignore routine maintenance. Over time, the wood had dried out and the holes around the metal had worn and widened. The rails were now distinctly rickety. Lady Waterbury had commented that they shook when Augustus handed her up to the seat. But her daughter, who was the only one who ever used the gig, since Augustus had always considered it beneath him, replied firmly, "It is perfectly safe, Mama. This gig was made of the finest materials. I still have the bill of sale. It was shockingly expensive."

Now, the poor horse trotted faster and faster, trying to rid himself of the irritant under his noseband, and when at last Mildred became aware of the speed at which they were going, she yanked on the reins, which drove the burrs even deeper into the horse's cheeks. He reared up. Completely unprepared, the ladies grabbed at the metal side rails. Weakened further by the shaking from the fast pace of the horse, and unaccustomed to the ferocity of the grasp and the weight of the frightened ladies, the oak splintered. The rails broke away from their moorings. Without their restraint, the ladies were tossed off the sides of the gig, one on one side, one on the other.

Lady Waterbury hit her head on a stone mile marker hidden by tall grasses at the side of the road and was killed instantly. Mildred was tumbled into a ditch, hard and dry after a hot summer, and broke three top ribs. The sharp end of one of them punctured her lung. The lung collapsed and the leaking air pressure on her heart caused cardiac arrest. She was dead in thirty minutes.

The horse, content to no longer have the irritating pressure from the reins, but still attached to the upturned vehicle, cropped peaceably at the grass not far from the dead lady Waterbury until a passing farmer came upon the grisly scene. He saw at once he could do nothing for the two women, tethered the horse and ran the mile or so to the Waterbury house.

Augustus was indoors but heard the hue and cry in the yard. He came running out, imagining his wife and mother-in-law had returned, complaining about the uncomfortable ride. When he heard what had happened, he had a horse saddled and was flying down the road in a matter of minutes, giving an excellent impression of a man suffering from deep distress. He wanted to remove the burrs, of course.

He arrived at the scene before anyone else and was able to find and remove the irritants at once. He then sat by the side of the road and dissolved into very real tears. The others, coming along a little later, were struck by his desolation and gave him every credit for a man bereaved. In fact, he was crying from shock, fear of discovery and relief.

For Augustus, the next few weeks went by in a haze. He discovered that in law when two people die in the same accident, the older is deemed to have died first. This was, in fact, the case with his wife and mother-in-law, though he did not know it. But it meant that the Dowager's possessions passed to her daughter, and the daughter's possessions passed to her husband. The grieving widower was suddenly a wealthy man. He now owned not only the estate in Berkshire and his wife's fortune, but also his mother-in-law's money and the house in London with its dark William and Mary furniture and its even darker portraits of the ancestors. In fact, he would one day figure amongst them.

For the first few weeks, he proceeded to get royally drunk every night, sleep most of the day and spend the rest of the daylight hours walking around saying to himself, "That's mine... and that... and that." As soon as it was seemly to do so, he summoned Colby and had him lay out in plain terms the extent of his fortune in terms of ready cash and investments. It was very substantial. He was delighted to see that he was master of a thriving concern. "Good old Mildred," he said to himself, raising a glass in her honor, "she certainly knew how to manage an estate!" But then it was borne in upon him that he did, too. He had followed her directions long enough that they had become second nature. And it was now all up to him. By God, he could do it!

He abruptly stopped drinking excessively, began to go to bed at a reasonable hour and get up betimes to do his rounds. If the tenants had been polite enough before, now they were positively obsequious. He was no kinder or more generous than Mildred had been, but they knew which side their bread was buttered. At the inn in the village, where they used to call him The Master with some irony, they now used the term in all sincerity. His stature amongst the available wenches was higher than ever. For some months, he had the time of his life.

By degrees, however, he began to think, as men of fortune will, where all this effort of management and husbandry would eventually go. What was it all for? He had no heir. There were a couple of children in the village who bore an unmistakable resemblance to him, but he was not interested in a son whose mother was a peasant. He decided to go back to London and try his luck again.

The season was in full swing when he arrived. He moved into the gloomy townhouse and spent hours looking in every nook and cranny muttering, *mine, mine*. He wasted no time visiting his tailor who, bowing so low his nose almost touched his knee, declared himself ready to furnish Mr. Protheroe with whatever he might require. He ordered several funereally dark outfits, meaning to milk his widowed status as much as he could.

He wanted a new high-perch phaeton, sniggering to himself that Mildred had never dreamed, when she claimed such a vehicle was useless in the country, that the lowly gig would be her undoing, but decided to hold off for the time being. Instead he ordered a smart new barouche, all in black, of course. He made the rounds of the gentlemen's clubs, renewed his acquaintance with his old cronies, lost money to them at cards with a sad little smile, and willingly paid for their drinks and dinners. Naturally enough, they thought him a stout fellow. Since most of them were by now married, they encouraged their wives to invite him to their soirées and parties. *Such a fine chap,* they all agreed. *Still mourning his dear wife.*

Chapter Twenty-Seven

Hastings 1814-1815

For a long time after her beloved husband's death, Claire was too heart-broken to think about anything more than getting through the day without him. She stopped making her home cures and shook her head when anyone applied to her for cupping. Héloise had seen her do it often enough and could take her place, but they were running out of the hyssop balm that accompanied it.

The finances of the inn had taken a turn for the worse. The revenue over the dreadful winter and delayed spring of 1814 had been way down. They had been forced to employ an extra man and scullery maid once things began to get back to normal, and now Héloise feared they might need a maid for the bedrooms. Claire would stop in the middle of re-making a bed, tears filling her eyes as she thought of how Bernard had made her laugh when he saw her performing these domestic chores. "Hmm, he would say, catching her around her waist from behind, "I always had fantasies concerning a maid in a white apron!"

It fell more and more to Héloise to keep the accounts and pay their suppliers. The money they had put away for Emile's education was dwindling to nothing. In fact they were using their reserves. She saw only too clearly what was happening, and racked her brains to think how she could make enough money to pay for her son's education and support the inn. She considered getting a job as a governess, but when she investigated the advertisements in the newspapers, she saw the wages were pitifully low. It would take her years to save enough to make a difference, and honestly, she didn't think she could bear to teach someone else's children while her own son was left at home.

One day, she was flicking idly through the romances she used to read, thinking how foolish she had been to imagine that love would conquer all, when the shocking idea came to her. She tried to put it from her mind at first, but gradually, as she confronted it, she began to think it had possibilities. She knew men paid for women, and from what she had heard her mother and father say from time to time, it was even a tradition in France for the king to have an official mistress. Those women were accepted at all levels of society.

She knew she was good-looking. Why should she not set herself up as a high-priced courtesan? The fact that she was French would make it all the more convincing. She realized she knew nothing of the arts of pleasing a man. Her dealings with Augustus had been nothing more than uncomfortable fumblings. But, like the scholar she had been, she thought there must be a book to describe such things.

"Non, non et non!" cried Claire, when she heard what her daughter was thinking. "You must be mad! Think what your poor father would say!"

She was less discouraged by the absolute negative of her mother than by her inability to find out what she needed to know. Under the pretext of looking for different texts, Héloise searched the vicar's bookshelves to no avail. It was not surprising, she told herself. Even if such manuals existed, they would hardly be in a vicar's possession. But it seemed as if fate was on her side.

That summer saw the arrival of one of the itinerant peddlers from France. This one was accompanied by his wife, a buxom, saucy-eyed wench who had her own way of adding to the family coffers, evidently with her husband's connivance, since he seemed the one organizing his wife's activities. They stayed at the inn for the night. Going upstairs to her room, Héloise heard giggling and a male voice coming from their bedchamber, when she knew the peddler was in the saloon drinking Calvados. She stayed in the shadows and saw a man leave the room, and a short while later, another arriving. This happened twice more before the peddler himself arrived and the giggling ceased.

The following morning, Héloise was up betimes and in the kitchen when the peddler came down for his breakfast.

"I shall take coffee up to Madame," she said to Agnès.

"Humph, Madame, is it? I've got another name for it," replied Agnès, who knew perfectly well what had gone on the previous evening. Joseph had told her, saying it was a good thing they were only staying one night, because otherwise he would have to put them out.

"This has always been a respectable establishment," he pronounced, "and for our late Monsieur's sake as well as our own it will remain so."

"Well then, the quicker she gets her coffee, the quicker they'll leave," said Héloise, taking the tray up the stairs.

She knocked on the door of the visitors' bedchamber and walked in, announcing, "Votre café, Madame."

153

The peddler's wife sat up in bed at the smell of the coffee. She was practically naked, with a dingy chemise barely covering her round breasts, and her almost black curls tumbling around her shoulders. Looking at her dispassionately, Héloise could see she had an allure deriving as much from her complete confidence in her own body as in her very obvious charms.

"Good morning, Madame," she began, then plunged on. "I hope you will not mind my mentioning I observed the comings and goings in this bedchamber last night."

"What of it?" asked the peddler's wife, suspiciously. More than once before an innkeeper had demanded a share of the profits in return for not going to the authorities.

But Héloise astonished her.

"I'm hoping, Madame," she said, "that you will instruct me a little in the arts of your... er profession."

She spoke in French, of course, since the woman's English was practically non-existent, but also because it seemed more appropriate, somehow.

Recovering from her surprise at being asked such a question by an apparently virtuous woman at such an early hour of the morning, Claudette, as her name turned out to be, was a fount of information.

"Just pour me out a cup of coffee, and sit down here," she said, patting the eiderdown on the bed. "First of all, tell me what you do know."

Héloise gave her the invented story: she had been briefly married but her husband had died in the wars. She hadn't had time to learn much.

"Well, the first thing to know is that men are nearly all only concerned with themselves and so long as you've got a pretty face and you're willing, they don't give a damn about anything else. Your most important job is to make the bloke feel he's a wonderful lover, and you'd go with him even if he wasn't paying," began Claudette. "Course, it's never true, or hardly ever. And take my advice: don't go with a man if you like him too much. That's what I did and look where it landed me. My old man got me all hot and bothered, so I married him and now I does the same job but has to share the money with him. And he don't care how I make it, so long as he gets me when he wants me."

She took a long sip of her coffee and continued. "The two things you'll have to deal with is either they're too fast, or they can't get it up. 'Course if they're too fast that's their own look-out. You gets paid the same. If you're feeling kindly you can help 'em a bit. If they can't get it up, it's best if you give 'em a hand or else they gets all weepy or angry. In any case, you makes 'em all pay in advance no matter what. But this is what you can do in either case, if you feel like it."

And she described techniques, various positions, and methods that professional women have known forever.

"But like I said," she ended, "the thing is, they're more concerned with themselves than you, so as long as you tell 'em how wonderful they are and pretend you're having a good time, they'll be 'appy." She stopped, and looked at Héloise curiously. "But you ain't goin' into the business, are yer? Lovely girl like you?"

"No," laughed Héloise. "I'm curious, that's all."

"Well," Claudette looked doubtful. "Just you look after yerself. Don't get yerself up the spout. Know what I mean? You know what to do?"

Héloise nodded. Yes, in that respect, she knew her mother would help her.

Chapter Twenty-Eight

London 1815

Once the peddlers had gone on their way, with many a friendly wave from Claudette, Héloise set to work persuading her mother that the plan she had formed was the only solution to their problems.

"Maman," she said, "just think for a minute. In the eyes of the world, I'm already a fallen woman. No man of honor will marry me. This is the only thing I can do to earn a great deal of money quickly. I have a plan that will enable me to earn enough in three years to send Emile to Eton and keep us all in reasonable comfort. Then we'll sell the inn and go to live in a quiet town far away where no one knows us. I shall become a respectable widow. After all these wars, that will be easily accepted. I've decided."

She was quiet for a moment, tapping her finger on her chin, utterly deaf to her mother's outrage. "Yes," she said, "I shall write to Lady Pevensey. She invited me years ago. Now I shall ask her to introduce me into society. She'll show me where to buy gowns and become an expensive lady. It's no good arguing, Maman, my mind is made up."

Claire's protests were in vain. Héloise was determined. In that way her daughter was just like her, though Claire didn't see it. In the end, the young woman had her way. Her mother gave her the jewelry she had sewn into the hem of her cloak all those years ago, and had kept, dreaming of her daughter wearing them at her wedding to a fine English gentleman. She gave her all the money she had saved. Then, at the last minute she wordlessly gave her a mixture she sold, or often gave, to the women in the village overburdened with five pregnancies in as many years. A complicated mixture of tansy, broom, rue, mugwort, wormwood, yarrow and pennyroyal, regular use as a tea would prevent a woman's monthly cycle. They had talked it all out, and no more words were necessary.

"We shall not tell Agnès and Joseph," declared Héloise "We'll just say I'm going to London to be a governess in a rich family. They would be even more horrified than you are."

It was true. In the class of society from which their old friends sprung, the sort of infidelities the upper classes readily accepted were not so easily swallowed. The result was that on the early summer day in 1815 when Joseph drove her to Dover to catch the London Mail, he chatted with her quite blithely about the well-placed family she pretended to be going to. Neither he nor Agnès wanted Héloise to go, of course. They hadn't been separated from her a day since she was born, but they understood her desire to educate her son the way her Papa had been educated. It was right, they told each other, for Emile to be a gentleman.

Héloise had written to Lady Pevensey to ask if she might stay for a few weeks, saying she had business affairs of her late father to attend to, and wanted to do some shopping. Her ladyship was delighted to receive her. With the death of her husband she stayed much closer to home, inviting just a few select friends now and then to very elegant card parties. But perhaps precisely because she was so selective, and because those she did invite were still very high flyers indeed, her position in the *ton* remained unassailable.

Moreover, she had not allowed her personal standards to fall, in spite of her relative seclusion. She had no desire to turn into an unfashionable dowager. Though she attended only a very few of the most select tonnish events, she did so in the very latest style. When her old dresser was pensioned off, she hired a new, younger one, who kept her finger on the pulse of fashion. Her name was Martha Skipton. She was sister to Augustus Protheroe's valet.

Lady Pevensey had not been to visit her brother since her husband died and knew nothing of the birth of Emile. She found she hated to travel without a man, and since her twin nephews had gone to Eton and then Oxford, she had kept up with family news by being their hostess whenever they were in London. Alice and Julian had also been much more in the capital with their boys. They had not felt it right to spread gossip about the young woman whom they had known from birth. It was therefore years since her ladyship had seen Héloise and had since received only the most superficial news of her.

"My dear!" she said when the young woman followed the butler into the salon, "Come in, come in! Here, let Wooton take your pelisse and bonnet. Let me look at you!" And the older woman, having embraced her, held her at arm's length. "Lord, what a beauty you've grown into! Who would have thought it? You used to be so thin!" And then, "But what an outmoded gown. We shall certainly see to that!" And she led her to a chair, calling for tea.

Héloïse decided she should come to the point of her visit right away. She did not want to abuse her ladyship's hospitality and then drop what she was sure would be a bombshell on her. But her journey to London had been long and fatiguing. So she gratefully drank her tea and nibbled a little cake while Lady Pevensey peppered her with questions about her family. She had not heard of Bernard's death, and was genuinely sorry.

"Such a gentleman, your dear father," she said. "You must all miss him dreadfully. I know Julian enjoyed nothing so much as a discussion with him. How does your poor mother go on?"

"She is still recovering from the shock," replied Héloïse quietly. "It's a blessing we have Emile…," she had allowed the name to slip out unthinkingly, and hesitated, but then decided this was the moment to explain it all.

"And so," she concluded after an unvarnished recitation of the facts. "To educate my son and give my mother the life she deserves, I have come to London to… to make money as quickly as possible in the only way a woman like me can. I hope you will help me to become a society lady and introduce me to the *ton*. After that, you may wash your hands of me. I perfectly understand you may abhor the idea, so I'm telling you this at once, my lady, so that you may show me the door, if you wish."

As we have seen, as a girl Lady Pevensey was of a very determined character. She had not been prepared for life to find her; she had found it. She had decided that life as the wife of an aristocrat would suit her, she had fixed on a Peer she could mold and she had set about marrying him. Her position in society had turned out exactly as she had planned, though now she very much missed her amiable spouse.

She recognized something of herself in Héloise. She thanked her lucky stars she had not been forced to make the sort of decision the young woman had had to make, but knew that had it been her only alternative, she would have done the same.

She therefore said to the young woman before her, "I don't abhor your decision. I understand your situation and I commend you for your courage. I am willing to do my best for you, not only for your own sake, but for the sake of my dear husband, who thought so highly of you. He spoke of you fondly till the day he died. Now, drink your tea and let's make plans."

And so began the second education of Héloise Rambuteau. Her ladyship entered into the affair with a determination that was quite like the old days. Luckily, she said, Héloise's excellent education had made her fit for any drawing room in the country. But she should quell her instinct to express herself too freely. She should listen more than speak. All she needed was a little town bronze, beginning with a new wardrobe.

She took her to her own modiste and ordered fashionable day dresses, walking dresses, evening dresses and ballgowns. These she insisted in paying for herself, saying it was little enough in repayment of the great service Héloise and her mother had rendered to her husband. She hired a dancing master who came to the house with a quiet little woman who nevertheless played the piano with great verve. Together they taught Héloise the latest dances, including the waltz. Although reluctant at first to allow any man to take her around the waist, she soon became exhilarated with the whirling movement and music. Besides, she admonished herself, if she was going to be a courtesan, she needed to become accustomed to a good deal more than a man's hand upon her waist.

By the end of the summer, all these preparations were complete. Lady Pevensey deemed Héloise ready for her first test: a small dance party at Lady March's. She suggested having the young woman's abundant curls shortened at the sides, so that they could be left to form natural ringlets, while the rest was drawn up onto the top of her head. Her ladyship's own dresser did her coiffure on the night of the dance party and then helped Héloise into a very becoming pale blue silk evening gown with a demi-train that did nothing to hide her curves. She wore her mother's diamond pendant and matching earrings. She looked what she was: a beautiful woman not in her first, or even second season.

Martha Skipton stood back and surveyed her handwork with pride. "You look a picture, Miss," she said. "A real picture. Her ladyship's taste never fails!"

"Thank you, Skipton," said Lady Pevensey, coming into the room. "Yes, I'm glad we chose that shade of blue. It becomes you admirably, my dear." Then, turning to the dresser, "Run along now, if you please. I'd like to speak to Miss Héloise for a moment."

The household staff had been instructed to call their guest by that name, since her French surname name was deemed unpronounceable.

As she left, Martha caught the end of her gown in the door and was forced to open it again to free it. While she was not particularly nosy, and was discretion itself about the various beauty aids her employer was nowadays forced to employ, she was halted in her tracks as she quietly closed the door the second time.

She heard her ladyship declare in her normal rather piercing tones, "Héloise, my dear, I think we shall introduce you as Mrs.

Ramsay. That way, should the existence of your son ever become known, it will be easy to explain that you are the widow of an English soldier who unfortunately met his end in the wars in Spain. Your boy is six years old, you say? Yes, that would fit. And Ramsay is a common enough name. Rambuteau is too... French."

Martha Skipton stopped short and opened her eyes wide. So, Miss Héloise had a son, six years old! Who would have thought it? She had the figure of a girl still! And the father was... well, who knew who the father was? She sighed. What a pity, for she was ever so pretty and kind, but how would she find a husband now? Who would want to marry a woman like that? And what was her real name? Some French thing, her ladyship had said. Began with an R, but God knows what the rest was. No wonder she stuck to Miss Héloise! She shook her head and went on her way. She didn't mention the matter to anyone in the household.

Thus it was that Héloise was introduced by Lady Pevensey to their hosts that evening as a widowed family friend who, now that her period of mourning was over, had come for a quiet visit to London. Her parents had been French émigrés. No one thought to question her credentials. She danced every dance but without ostentation. She drew no attention to herself. She engaged in very ladylike conversation with her hostess and the other worthy ladies in the room. If a gentleman spoke to her, she answered quietly and with dignity, looking him right in the eyes as if he were the only man present. At the end of it, one and all declared her a very pretty-behaved young woman and vowed to leave calling cards for her at Lady Pevensey's. Her first social engagement had been a triumph.

The invitations came thick and fast and she was received everywhere. She was given vouchers for Almack's, though she never used them. Héloise was too wise to subject herself to the ostracizing by the patronesses she was sure would soon come. They had once refused entry to the Duke of Wellington himself simply for being improperly dressed.

Before long it was known that Mrs. Ramsay had decided to stay in London, where people were so kind and the society so refined. It was reported she had taken a small house on the edge of Mayfair, though she received no one there. Then the intelligence gradually emerged that she did receive guests, but only men, a different one every three months, and they paid handsomely for the privilege. A few of the very high sticklers ceased inviting her, but the men who paid for her company were themselves of the highest *ton* and it was impossible to refuse them, so she was still seen everywhere. Her behavior continued exemplary: her conversation was good, her bearing regal. It was not long before comparisons were made with the very aristocratic mistresses of the Courts of France. Just as Héloise had said, being French explained everything.

Chapter Twenty-Nine

London 1816

Having received his last refusal from Mrs. Ramsay, for a while Rory Compton continued his wild spree with every other available female, but after a couple of months tired of the meaninglessness of it all. Both he and the women concerned knew they were engaging in uncommitted amusement, nothing more. Then, though the comparison would have disgusted him, like Augustus Protheroe he found himself contemplating his future, and thought perhaps the time had come for him to marry.

It was his mother who started it. "Rory, dear," she gently chided him one day, "they tell me you've now dropped Bess Crawford and are seen with Sally Ripton. How many is that this month?"

When he muttered something in response she continued, "You know I've never scolded you and I don't propose to start now, but just think, my dear! You are of an age when you should be thinking of marrying and setting up your nursery. All your friends have done so! Consider what will happen if you die without an heir."

While he was annoyed at being put on the spot like this, he knew she was right. Her words brought home to him the importance of securing the family name. He had no brothers, and should he die without issue, the title would go to a cousin he particularly disliked. The man was a mushroom! He collected little plates or some such. Imagine the name of Dexter associated with a room full of china!

"What, you, Rory?" exclaimed one of his friends when he mentioned what was on his mind. "Never say it! You're the last of us not to be leg-shackled. Who're we to look up to if you succumb?"

"Oh, stow it, Barney," he replied. "Don't tell me you aren't glad to go home to the old lady of an evening and hear the patter of tiny feet in the nursery."

"Well, it's all right, I suppose," said his friend a little reluctantly. "Does you good to see the family line continued, and all that. My little fella's a right one. You'll never guess what he said to me the other day!"

And Barney proceeded to tell him a story of his offspring's brilliance that only the proud Papa could find interesting. Yes, there was nothing for it, decided Lord Dexter, but to marry and produce an heir so he could tall tales of his own.

The unmarried women in high society London fell into three categories. The first was the debutantes of the year: nearly always pretty as girls of that age are, often lovely, some with money, all looking for a husband both rich and handsome. The second was the slightly less well-endowed young women who had come out last year but had been unable to fix the attentions of a gentleman who was both rich and handsome. They were now willing to settle for one or the other. Third the young women who were into their third season and by now were ready to settle for any husband at all. There was, of course, a fourth category: those who had been out for even longer without any luck in the marriage stakes. These were approaching or firmly in the status of Old Maid. For them, all hope was lost, and the best they could hope for was to go home and be a Prop to Mama or a fond aunt to their luckier sisters' children.

Lord Dexter liked women and women liked him. He was fairly sure he could have his pick. He looked around at the first two of the aforementioned categories, hoping to find what he was looking for in their ranks. He approached several potential mates as subtly as he could, so as not to raise expectations in any maidenly breast.

But at the end of these forays he was no further ahead. Any one of them would probably do, he thought, except he found them all such a dead bore. What was it about virtuous, well-bred young women that robbed them of anything interesting to say? They had no conversation. To sit with them was to hear *yes Lord Dexter*, or *no Lord Dexter*, or occasionally, by way of a change, *I really couldn't say, Lord Dexter*.

The only woman who held any attraction for him was Mrs. Héloise Ramsay. She had just come to the end of her latest engagement. Bryce Woolston had succeeded Ferdy Carrington. He was the grandson of an enormously rich mill owner and though some of the highest sticklers maintained he still smelled of the shop, his education at Harrow and Cambridge and his very deep pockets made him acceptable to most of the *ton*. His three months were nearly up.

But though she would acknowledge Rory with a slight inclination of the head, she otherwise ignored him. Damn her. He knew her pattern well enough by now. When her latest protector's term of office (as he termed it to himself) came to an end, she would disappear for a few weeks before reappearing with a new one.

He was therefore surprised when almost immediately after Woolston's tenure was over, she appeared on the arm of a Major Beresford, a good-looking fellow in full regimentals. The women clustered about him, so handsome in his uniform, and the men enjoyed listening to his accounts of the military engagements chasing Bonaparte on the Continent. Mrs. Ramsay said he was an old friend, but neither of them was forthcoming with any details.

Rory didn't believe it. He thought she had found herself a new man, though God knows where he got the money. He certainly wouldn't get paid anything like the sum she required in the Army. He must come from a wealthy family. Jealousy smote him like a sword, and he found he could hardly be civil to the fellow.

In anger and frustration, he cast his eye around again. It fell upon Philippa Warner. She was a very handsome young woman in her third season. There was no reason why she shouldn't have "taken" except that she was extremely proper, humorless, and often found to be reading moral tracts by Hannah Moore and William Wilberforce. She was, furthermore, strictly opposed to the consumption of alcohol and any sort of gambling or profligacy. The only interesting aspect of this, as far as Lord Dexter was concerned, was that she was prepared to talk to him about it all. He amused himself trying to find chinks in her armor or presenting more and more convoluted moral dilemmas for her to untangle in her evenly delivered discourse.

Deciding that having something to talk about was better than nothing, he proposed to her a few weeks later. She looked at him calmly and said, "You will, of course, talk to my father. But you may tell him I shall consent to a betrothal, Lord Dexter, on certain

168

conditions. If you are able to demonstrate that you have put aside the... wildness of your past life, you may be a suitable husband for me. During our engagement I do not expect to hear that you have been engaged in horseracing, pistol shooting, boxing, or ridiculous wagers, or any activities that might bring discredit upon my family. I do not talk of yours, though I daresay your dear mother has often had cause to regret your wild behavior."

Since, it was at his mother's urging that he had decided to settle down, he merely bowed, smiled, and muttered "of course." In fact, he knew she adored him and though she had often mentioned his wild behavior over the years, it was only because she was afraid there was a too much of his father in him. She had only ever remonstrated gently about his behavior and had never made him feel she loved him a jot the less for it.

"I understand," continued his chosen one, "it was quite the thing for you and your cronies to be taken up by the Watch in the early hours and spend the night in goal before appearing before the Magistrate, giving a false name and simply paying a fine."

"My dear Miss Warner, or may I call you Philippa?" he smiled, "I assure you that those days are far behind me. Indeed, I wonder that you, of all people, should be aware of such things."

"Nor do I expect to see you drinking spirituous liquors," continued his chosen one, as if he had not spoken. "And it goes without saying," she continued, "that your involvement with opera singers or other women of low morals has to end."

"Naturally, Philippa," he smiled.

"I prefer we keep the formalities, Lord Dexter. Please call me Miss Warner until we are both sure of this... connection."

"All I expect is a son and heir, and a woman I can talk to. She can expect what she pleases," said Rory to himself. "Once we are married I shall do what I damned well want. Not the opera singers, of course, but if I want to have a drink or bet on the horses, I shall."

But these thoughts remained, of course, unspoken. All he said was, "Of course, my dear Miss Warner."

Chapter Thirty

London 1816

When Augustus Protheroe began to haunt the salons of the rich and famous once again, it was not long before he heard the name Héloise Ramsay. Over the years, he had completely forgotten her. But when he saw Héloise, his memory stirred. Where had he seen that face before? He passed in review his various conquests until suddenly he thought he knew. Wasn't that the girl he'd had down in—where was it? Hastings. Yes, that was it. She'd been a remarkably pretty piece and well educated. Not your run-of-the-mill country chit. He remembered a girl eager to please, with wide, trusting eyes. Could this beautiful, elegant, and composed woman be her? How many Héloises could there be in England? But he didn't approach her and she didn't seem to notice him.

He asked about her in his club.

"La Belle Ramsay?" said one of his cronies. "She appeared out of nowhere last year. Friend of Lady Pevensey, no less. She's available—if you're lucky, and rich enough. Five thousand for three months, apparently."

Augustus whistled.

"Yes, and she's been known to turn down some of the most eligible fellows. She refused Rory Compton, if you can believe it. At the moment she's got that Major fellow. They say they're just friends, but no one's such a flat as to believe that. Anyway, the *on-dit* is he's leaving next week, so you can try your luck—if you've got the blunt."

"I've got the blunt, all right, but I don't know if I'd give that for any piece of skirt. Besides what I want is a wife young enough to give me an heir and do as she's told. La Ramsay is a nice-looking armful but...."

"The fellows who've had her claim she's a piece of perfection. Anyway, plenty of girls about. Shouldn't be too hard to find one."

"Not going to rush into anything. Been down that road before."

In truth, Augustus did not really want to marry again at all. He'd had enough of that with Mildred. No matter how compliant they may seem before marriage, wives either turned into harridans, chivvying their husbands over the slightest little thing, or a waterworks, crying they didn't love them anymore because a lightskirt happened to take their fancy.

But he did want an heir, someone to carry on his name. Still, perhaps he'd have a bit of fun before settling down. The Ramsey woman had stirred his interest. She'd refused Rory Compton, had she? That made him smirk. When Augustus had been in London before, he'd been forced to take on Mildred, while the high flyers who wouldn't even give him the time of day had flocked to Lord Dexter. He'd hated him then. It would be sweet revenge to have a woman Dexter couldn't have.

But five thousand pounds! No woman was worth that! If he said he remembered her, she'd have to come off her high horse, wouldn't she? She wouldn't want the *ton* to know she was just a landlady's daughter from an inn in Hastings. But for reasons he didn't bother to analyze, he didn't really want to tell anyone about their affair. He was convinced that if he threatened to talk she'd drop her price.

A week later there was a farewell party for Major Beresford and the field was clear for Augustus. But Héloise, who was still in her "rest" period between gentlemen, was not to be seen at any of the parties or soirées he attended over the next week. Frustrated, he asked around in his clubs and found out her address. He didn't want his smart barouche to be recognized, so he took a hackney to the little house in Mayfair. It was the middle of the afternoon on a fine autumn day. Just the sort of weather it had been when they met, he said to himself, in a rare moment of nostalgia.

At his knock, she opened the door and faced him calmly. He didn't know she'd had a judas installed in her front door, and she'd known who was standing there. She had hesitated, wondering whether to simply pretend she was not at home, but decided, after a moment's reflection, to open the door. At the party where he'd noticed her, she had recognized him, too, and had stifled a shock of fear. She had asked a few acquaintances about him and no one had much good to tell her. His loveless marriage and the shocking death of his wife and mother-in-law were well known to the *ton*, for servants always talked. In spite of his money, or because of how he had acquired it, he was thought to be a bad lot. She had guessed he would make himself known to her, one way or the other.

"May I help you, sir?" she said politely but coolly.

"Héloise, my dear!" cried her visitor. "Don't say you don't recognize me! It's your Augustus!"

"I'm sorry?" replied Héloise, with hauteur. "I have no idea who you may be. I was awaiting Lady Pevensey, that is why I answered the door myself. I think you must have the wrong address." And she made as if to close the door.

Augustus swiftly put his foot in the way. "Come now, Héloise! You must remember me! The delightful, er, interlude we enjoyed in Hastings in the autumn of, when was it? 1807?"

In fact, it was 1808, and Emile was born the following year. A vice clutched Héloise's heart as she thought of her son, but not for a moment did she waver.

"Sir," she said coldly. "Nothing you say has any meaning for me. I beg you to remove your foot from the door. I do not want to have my manservant run for the constable, but I shall do so if you continue to importune me in this manner."

And she called over her shoulder to a non-existent attendant, "Jackson, come here if you please."

"No need for that, no need for that," muttered Augustus, considerably put out. The interview had not gone in the least as he expected. He removed his foot and the door was summarily shut in his face. He rather shamefacedly descended the front steps and stood looking up at the tall narrow building before planting his hat, which he had removed to address Héloise, firmly on his head. He needed time to reconsider.

A day or so later, he was preparing for an evening out when Skipton, his valet, reminded him that the following day he would be absent. He was spending his day off with his sister.

"Sister?" said his master, idly filing his nails, "I had no idea you had a sister."

"Yes, sir," said Skipton. "She is dresser to Lady Pevensey, a most advantageous position."

"Lady Pevensey?" said Augustus, sitting up straight. That was the name the Ramsey woman had mentioned. Come to think of it, the fellow in the club last week had said she'd been sponsored by someone of that name. "I say, Skipton," he said, "there's a fiver in it for you if you can find out something for me."

"Certainly sir, I'll do my possible." Skipton's attitude towards his master, at least to his face, had undergone a change since his unexpected inheritance.

"You've perhaps heard of a, er... lady by the name of Héloise Ramsay?"

"The name has been mentioned once or twice in my hearing. A very beautiful woman, I understand." Skipton was perfectly well aware of Mrs. Ramsay and her profession.

"Hmm." Augustus was non-committal. "Anyway, it seems she was introduced to the *ton* only last year by Lady Pevensey. Now, what I want to know is, where did she come from? I think she may have been, er, at school with dear Mildred and may like to know the details of her... accident."

Knowing very well how things had stood between his master and his late wife, and indeed, being the source of much of the information circulating amongst the *ton* about his master, Skipton was unconvinced by this explanation. But he *was* convinced by the offer of five pounds to find out what Augustus wanted to know.

The next day, therefore, he interrogated his sibling while strolling around the park. It was a beautiful autumn day, and they had decided to enjoy the last of the good weather before having a bite to eat and going to see a farce in Drury Lane. He was proud of his sister Martha. She was nice-looking and the excellent taste that made her a good lady's dresser was reflected in her own attire.

"Gusty Protheroe (which is how he referred to his employer in his absence) has his eye on a woman called Héloïse Ramsay. Apparently she's a friend of your old widow. D'you know anything about her?"

"Oh, Petey (for Skipton's first name Peter), you didn't ought t'call her my old widow! She's a dear soul, for all she's got her own ideas about everything. It's a good position for me, y' know."

"She's lucky to have you, you mean. Every other dresser I've ever clapped eyes on has looked like a pickled herring!"

His sister laughed. "Oh, go on, you flatterer! Anyway, what do you want to know about Mrs. Ramsay? One thing I can tell you, that's not her real name. It was some French thing. I dunno what it was, 'cept it began with an R. We always called her Miss Héloïse."

"What d'you mean? Always called her?"

"She stayed with us for quite a time when she first come to London. Though," she hesitated, "She don't come to the house these days."

Martha hesitated again. "I overheard them talking and it seems... well, it seems Miss Héloïse had a son. Seven years old he is! You'd never think it, to look at her, would you? She don't look old enough! Anyway, they was going to say her husband was killed in the wars. But it's my belief she never had no husband. Poor thing! As pretty as she is, and all! She'll never get one, now."

"It don't seem she's looking for a husband. I hear she's a high-class working woman, if you get my drift."

Martha's eyes grew round as she looked at her brother. "So it's true!" she said. "That was the word going around but I didn't believe it. Who'd ever have thought it? She was so nice! Always a please and thank-you, and a real pleasure to dress! Such a lovely figure! And her a friend of my lady. It don't make any sense."

"Makes sense to me. A looker like her wouldn't give old Gusty the time of day otherwise. But he can pay, now he's got the dibs. Anyway, he said he'd give me a fiver for what I could find out. So next time I sees you, I'll treat you to a slap-up dinner."

And brother and sister walked along, arm in arm, Héloise forgotten as they discussed where they would go for dinner courtesy of Augustus Protheroe.

Chapter Thirty-One

London 1816

When Augustus heard what Skipton had to tell him, he surprised the valet by sitting back in his chair with an odd smile on his face and saying, "By God, that's mighty interesting, Skipton. Good work! A son, seven years old, you say. Now, I wonder...?"

"I'm glad to give satisfaction, sir," replied his valet, with a bow. "If I may remind you of the, er... fiver you promised?"

"Did I? Well, if you say so." Pulled from his reverie, Augustus reluctantly took his billfold from his waistcoat pocket and opened it. He rifled through the notes and then said, "Sorry, Skipton. Seems I don't have a fiver on me." He reached into the pocket of his buff-colored pantaloons that his man knew had cost him all of six guineas, and gave him a handful of coins. "Here, that should cover it."

It didn't, of course, but the valet reflected he should have known his master would never keep his word. When had he ever?

So, Héloïse had a child, did she? A seven-year-old son. Well, that would fit, right enough. Augustus took a day to consider what he should do next. Should he ride straight down to Hastings? But why waste the time and money if it turned out that either Skipton's sister had it wrong, or the child, if he existed, was not seven years old at all? After all, he was the first man to have the wench, but obviously not the last.

No, if the child was his, his best bet was to make the woman admit it. Then, if he liked the look of the boy, he could claim him as his son and have the heir he wanted without the expense and uncertainty of marrying anyone. He might keep the Ramsay woman on the hook, though. She'd probably be happy to do anything he wanted to get a look at the boy now and then. And there was no denying she was a fine-looking woman. Refused Dexter, had she? Well, she wouldn't refuse him! He went to sleep that night well pleased with himself. *A stroke of good fortune*, he thought, *at last!*

The next morning, having decided he didn't want to risk being left on Héloise's front steps like last time, he wrote her a note.

> *Dear Mrs. Ramsay, (though I have reason to*
> *believe that's not your real name),*
> *When I visited you a few days ago you denied any*
> *acquaintance with me and shut the door in my face.*
> *I think you will not do so this time. I have just*
> *learned about a certain young relative you have in*
> *Hastings. I believe he may be closely related to me.*
> *I'm sure we can do business. I shall be at your*
> *address at two o'clock tomorrow afternoon to*
> *discuss what next steps may be taken.*
> *Yours, etc.*
> *Augustus Protheroe*

Héloise's heart leaped into her throat when she received the note. She had to clutch the edge of the console table in the hall to steady herself. How had Protheroe found out about Emile? She had spoken about her son to no one in London except Lady Pevensey, and she was sure her ladyship would have nothing to do with a man like Augustus. When she was able to maintain her equilibrium, she paced around the little house, thinking furiously. Then she rang the bell to call the husband and wife team who were her only servants.

"Mr. and Mrs. Perkins," she said as calmly as she could when they presented themselves, "I'm leaving London for an indefinite period. I want you to take the knocker off the door and close the shutters on the front of the house. If anyone should come looking for me, tell them I'm away and you don't know where I've gone or when I'll be back. This is no less than the truth, as I do not propose to tell you. The lease is settled for another eighteen months and I shall pay your wages as normal. I may or may not be back in that time. If not, I shall write with instructions."

She took a deep breath, "Mr. Perkins, I need you to go and hire a carriage with reliable horses and a driver who is prepared for a long trip to...," she invented, "... to the west country. Thank you both. I know I can count on you not to talk of this to anyone."

Héloise had never seen the point of buying a carriage, with the cost of maintaining the horses, stabling and grooms. She had lived simply, saving as much money as she could. But now she regretted it. If she had a carriage, she would already be gone. At all costs, she must get to Hastings and hide Emile before Protheroe got there. She had only earned half of what she had hoped to earn, but it would have to be enough. No sacrifice was too great to prevent her son falling into the hands of the man who had ruined her.

Lady Pevensey, ever practical, had put her in touch with her own man of business, and Héloise now wrote to him, giving him her address in Hastings and asking him to arrange banking for her at the closest location, as well as the continued payment of her servants. He was also to return the sum of five thousand pounds to Sir Harry Brothers, who was to have been her next client. She next wrote to Sir Harry himself, explaining she was unable to keep her contract with him, and that his payment would be returned. He would be none too pleased, she thought ruefully, but it couldn't be helped.

She managed by force of willpower to complete these practical matters, but when she no longer had them to occupy her, she found she was trembling with fear. Finally, after chewing the end of her pen and beginning and destroying the letter three times, she wrote to Rory Compton, Lord Dexter.

Dear Lord Dexter,

I hesitate to write to you, but I believe you to be my friend.

I am leaving London immediately for Hastings. That is where I was born and raised.

My parents were French émigrés who, though it was not the life they had been born to, took over the ownership of an inn there called The Traveller's Rest.

It is there that Augustus Protheroe took advantage of my innocence when I was a girl and left me carrying his child.

My reason for this precipitous departure is that I believe my young son is in danger from his father, who up till now was ignorant of his existence. He now wishes to claim him, and in law, he has the right to do so. But this is something I will do everything in my power to prevent.

It is for my son that I have become what I am, to earn the money to give him the education his birthright deserves. My dear father and mother left their homeland for these shores in the hopes of giving me a better future. I destroyed their hopes for me with my foolishness. My father died eighteen months ago. I will not now let his memory be sullied by allowing his grandson to be ripped from his family and brought up by a coward and a poltroon.

Apart from my mother and a beloved working couple who have lived with us all my life, there is no one to protect Emile and me. I know I have brought this upon myself, but my son is blameless. You were once kind enough to say that if ever I needed your help you would be at my service. I need you now and I beg you to help us.

I know I have always refused your offers, but I give you my word that if you come to Hastings and let it be seen that I am under your protection, I will do whatever you desire. I do not believe Protheroe will dare stand up to you.

With grateful thanks, I am,
Héloise Rambuteau (Ramsay)

Héloise cried hot tears over this missive and nearly threw it in the rubbish, but she knew she would need more protection than poor Joseph could provide. He was no longer a young man, and she could not bear to see him beaten, or worse, by Augustus Protheroe. She had no choice; it was all she could do. In the end, she sealed it and gave it to Mr. Perkins for delivery that day along with the other letters, when he returned with a carriage and driver.

It was less than an hour later, and still only early afternoon, when Héloise was on her way to Hastings. With just two horses, the journey would take longer than with the Mail Coach, but she knew she would never get a place on the Mail without booking in advance. It would still take about 7 hours and need at least three changes of horses.

She should be there a full day before Augustus, presuming that the following afternoon he would be told she was gone, guess where she was, and follow her. It was possible, she supposed, that he would give up the attempt, but she thought he was probably stubborn enough to follow through with it.

Perkins had done well in his choice of carriage and driver, whose name turned out to be Alf. He was a taciturn fellow and merely grunted when she told him they were going, not to the West Country, but to Hastings. The pair of chestnuts he drove were strong animals, not beautiful, but with small heads and powerful shoulders. The carriage was old but well sprung and clean. To judge from the traces of a coat of arms still discernible on the doors, it had once belonged to an aristocratic family. The squabs were faded and mildly stained, but Héloise didn't notice as she sat back against them, her mind still in a whirl.

Why had she written to Rory Compton? She sat there and tried to think. She knew the reason she had consistently refused him was not because she didn't want him, but because she wanted him too much. The advice from Claudette had been categorical in that respect, and she was right. She knew she wouldn't be able to show him the door as she had so easily done the others.

She knew he'd been paying marked attention to Philippa Warner and whispers of an engagement had struck a knife into her heart. How foolish she was! But it was an odd choice. Philippa seemed such a cold fish, the total opposite of Rory himself. Surely he wasn't just playing a game with the young woman? Instinctively she knew he would not, just as she had instinctively trusted him when he said he would be of service to her.

But now she was regretting revealing her secret. His affections were engaged elsewhere. At best, he would respond to her note that he was sorry, but unable to help. At worst, he would throw it on the fire. She wouldn't blame him.

Alf the driver proved his worth once they stopped to change horses. She had ordered a cup of tea and when it came, it was scalding hot. She was trying to sip at it as she saw him shake his head decisively at a pair of horses even she could tell were broken down. She couldn't hear what he said to the ostlers in the din of the yard, but in a few moments they were back with a better looking pair. They were quickly poled up and ready to go. She fully expected Alf to take the time to drink a tankard of beer the ostlers handed him, but he did not. He took one gulp, handed it back and clicked up the new pair.

They stopped once more, made good time, and then descended to walk the horses up the steepest climbs up the High Weald. The sun set away to their right, casting swords of gold through the gaps between the ancient trees. As they trotted over the hill into Hastings, they rode into a night of stars.

Chapter Thirty-Two

London 1816

"Do you really think she'll be a suitable wife for you, Rory dear?" His mother turned to Lord Dexter with a look of concern. "I know her, or at least, I know *of* her. She's handsome, of course, and she seems very... very *good*, but... well, frankly, she's not who I imagined you marrying."

"Perhaps not, Mama. But at least she has some conversation. I find her views quite entertaining."

"*Entertaining*? But I understand she's opposed to alcohol in any form, speaks openly against hunting and horseracing...."

"And reads interminably from books of sermons," completed her son. "I know. But when she tells me why feels how she does, on the one hand I find myself examining my own conscience, which you must agree is a good thing, and on the other, imagining all sorts of moral dilemmas with which to confront her. She's always up to the challenge. I find it most stimulating."

His mother looked at him narrowly, not sure he wasn't making a joke. One never knew with Rory. He presented such a smiling, even temper to the world, one was inclined to think he took nothing very seriously. She knew this was not true. From time to time he had spoken to her about social ills and there were a number of charities he quietly supported, though no one but she and his man of business knew of it.

"Anyway," he said, smiling at her, "I thought you'd be glad. You're the one who told me I must marry. And just think what a good character the next Lord Dexter will be, if he takes after his mother."

"You know I only want you to be happy, my dear," she smiled back. "Any woman who has you as a husband will be very lucky."

"How can you say that, Mama?" he returned with a laugh, "when I don't know how many times you've rung a peal over me for my opera singers, ballet dancers, gambling, poor choice of friends and innumerable other faults."

"But I know at bottom you are a good person. You are kind and thoughtful. Look how you take care of me!"

"That's because if I don't, I'll find you swept away by some cavalier who will think you as beautiful as I do. If I could, I'd marry you myself!"

"Silly boy!" said his Mama fondly. "Anyway, if you think Philippa Warner is the one for you, then I will accept her with open arms."

"Perhaps not with open arms, Mama," said her son with a chuckle. "I don't think she likes hugging."

On the same day Héloise received the note from Protheroe indicating he knew of the existence of his son, Lord Dexter found himself in his carriage with his intended, on their way to make the formal request of Philippa's father for her hand in marriage. Unfortunately, it turned out Miss Warner was far too well bred to travel alone with a man, and brought along a duenna, a Miss Andrews, a pudding-faced woman of indeterminate age, who, when introduced, gave a brief curtsey, muttered something, and otherwise maintained a stony silence. The presence of this woman in the carriage prevented what Rory was hoping would be a tête à tête. He had told his mother he didn't think his intended liked hugging, but he was a man of considerable address and experience with women, and he had counted on breaking through her reserve.

As soon as she was seated, Philippa took a slim volume out of her reticule and began reading it. When he inquired as to the nature of her book, she replied "It is Fordyce's sermon on Female Virtue."

"Do you never read a novel, Miss Warner?"

"Definitely not. In fact, it is interesting you should bring that up. I am just reading Fordyce's words on that very subject. Would you like to hear what he says?

"With pleasure," he smiled.

She did not return his smile but began to read:

> We consider the general run of Novels as utterly unfit for you. Instruction they convey none. They paint scenes of pleasure and passion altogether improper for you to behold, even with the mind's eye. Their descriptions are often loose and luscious in a high degree; their representations of love between the sexes are almost universally overstrained. All is dotage, or despair. A sweet sensibility, a charming tenderness, a delightful anguish, exalted generosity, heroic worth, and refinement of thought; how seldom are these best ingredients of virtuous love mixed with any

judgment or care in the composition of their
principal characters!

"Do I understand then, Miss Warner," said Lord Dexter, "that you do not consider being in love a moment for extreme emotion, as your Fordyce expresses it: of *either despair or dotage?*"

"No," she said decidedly. "There should be no need for such extremes. One should neither dote nor be in despair."

"But what if the object of the doting does not return the feeling? Would that not lead to despair?"

"If one avoids the doting, one avoids the despair," she said succinctly.

"So you believe one may control love?"

"Most certainly."

"Ah, then you have never loved, to use the French expression, *à corps perdu?*"

"No."

"Pity," said Rory under his breath. Out loud he said, "Neither had Fordyce, apparently."

A few moments of silence passed. Philippa returned to her book. Then Rory said, "Miss Andrews, kindly change places with me." When that lady had climbed into the carriage she had not, as Rory had hoped, sat opposite Miss Warner, but next to her. With a startled look at Philippa, reassured by a slight nod, the duenna moved to the other side of the carriage. Rory took her place and slid down the banquette close to his intended. She shrank towards the side of the carriage. The very masculine presence so close to her was far from welcome. He took her hand, and kissed it.

"I should like to feel," he said in a low voice, "that you regarded me with something more than a *charming tenderness*, to use another one of the expressions from your Fordyce."

"Really, Lord Dexter," she said, withdrawing her hand, "He's not *my* Fordyce. Any young woman of refinement may take his words as a model. And as *for charming tenderness*, I see nothing wrong with it. No doubt with time and familiarity it may grow into a deeper feeling of mutual respect and esteem, but I do not look for more than that at the outset."

Rory sighed and moved away. So that was it. The most he could hope for was a charming tenderness and, if he was lucky, mutual respect and esteem. He suddenly thought of Héloise Ramsay. For some reason, he was quite sure that if she loved, it would not be with that lackluster emotion. For her it would be dotage and despair. For him too, he decided. His mother was right. Philippa was not the one for him. How the hell was he going to get out of this mess?

Chapter Thirty-Three

Hastings 1816

"I'm sorry, sir, Madame is from home," Mrs. Perkins made as if to close the front door on Augustus Protheroe who was keeping his two o'clock rendezvous. It was raining lightly.

"One minute, my good woman," he said, once again placing his foot against the door. "When do you expect her back?"

"I couldn't tell you, sir, not for fifty pounds, I couldn't," replied the lady. "She didn't say where she was going nor when she'd be back. Packed her bag and off she went."

"Hmm…." Augustus removed his foot and Mrs. Perkins gratefully closed the door. Augustus stood in the drizzle and pondered for a moment. Gone away with a bag. Knocker off the door. Shutters closed. Looked like she was gone for a while. And as Héloise expected, he guessed she must have gone to Hastings. Well, two could play at that game.

The minute he was home, he ordered the carriage to be brought round. He wouldn't take the barouche; in spite of the retractable canvas roof it would be damp and, anyway, if there was any sort of a struggle bringing the boy back, an enclosed vehicle would make it easier.

The carriage that drew up about half an hour later was the heavy, old fashioned affair his mother-in-law had used. She didn't believe in spending money unnecessarily (for which, in light of his handsome inheritance, he now thanked her), and had never thought to buy a new, more streamlined vehicle. It was ponderous and slow, but very comfortable, and as he sank back against the squabs and pulled a heavy blanket over his knees, unlike Héloïse a little over twenty-four hours before, Augustus was perfectly calm. He lay back, happy to be a man of means, and looking forward to achieving his aims. The Ramsay woman would have no alternative but to hand the boy over. He was his by right, in law. He might bring her back too, if he felt like it. She could help settle the boy in and provide himself with entertainment. Once the lad was in school, well, he'd see.

The driver was not happy to be starting a long journey in the afternoon, and in the rain. Grumbling, he whipped up the horses. He tried to push them along, but long accustomed to the sedate pace set by her ladyship, and pulling the heavy vehicle, they soon settled back into their slow trot. From his frequent visits to his uncle, Augustus was well acquainted with the road. He knew it took about seven hours. He was by nature indolent, and snoozing in the comfortable carriage suited him. It shouldn't be much past ten when he got there. He'd have them give him a bit of supper, secure the boy in his own room and tomorrow morning at a reasonable hour, bring him back to London. It would be easy.

But he reckoned without the slow pace of her late ladyship's horses and the discontent of the driver, who had been looking forward to a dinner when they stopped in Sevenoaks to change the horses. But they were turned away everywhere they went. No room! No room! Like Claire and Bernard all those years ago in Normandy, he had happened upon market day. The farmers, who had started out before dawn that morning, were all enjoying a well-earned meal. Not a table to be had. Augustus gave up at last, and at the final inn they visited where no table was available he drowned his hunger with a mug of the house porter, for which it was famous. The driver drowned his with two.

It was a strong drink, nicknamed Triple Stout. This went not only to the driver's head but also to his bladder. He was forced to stop along the road more than once to answer an urgent call of nature, then felt increasingly sleepy and all but dropped the reins. The rainclouds covered the stars. Apart from the narrow beams of their own lamps, the road was pitch black. The new horses, already off kilter because of the unaccustomed weight of the carriage and the lack of direction from the reins, started at the sounds and scamperings of small animals. More than once it was only because they were going so slowly that they missed being tumbled into a ditch. Consequently, it was almost midnight before they drew up in front of *The Traveller's Rest*.

Hearing the carriage, Joseph came to the door and stood in the half-opened doorway, a big man, his arms crossed, effectively blocking the entrance.

"Good evening, my man," said Augustus, with an attempt at bonhomie. "I'm looking for Héloise Ramsay."

"I don't know about a Ramzee," responded Joseph, "but Mademoiselle Héloise isn't here. She lives in London nowadays." his French accent was still noticeable, though his English was fluent.

"Well then, have her boy brought before me." Augustus thought it was possible Héloise hadn't come home, after all. That made it even easier.

"Her boy? What boy? There's no boy here."

"Look, my good fellow. Don't play the idiot with me. I know Héloise whatever her name is has a son. He's mine. I wish to see him."

"And I'm telling you there's no boy here. Come in if you like," replied Joseph with a thin smile. "See if you can find a boy anywhere." He stepped aside a little and Augustus pushed by him.

There was a comfortable fug of smoke and beer in the low-pitched room, overlaid with the scent of something delicious. Five or six men were sitting around, their collars open, their ruddy faces flushed.

"This gentleman is looking for a boy," announced Joseph.

"What boy would that be, then?" asked someone.

"My son. He's about seven years old."

"What's e' look like?"

"Well, there you have me. I'm not sure. But I'll know him if I see him."

"What's 'is name?"

"Ah, well, again, I couldn't rightly say."

"So yer lookin' fer a boy wot's yer son, but y' don't know what 'e looks like nor wot 'is name may be?"

"Yes, I know it sounds...."

But Augustus had no time to finish for there was a shout of laughter from the men and then someone called, "Any road, there ain't no boy 'ere. But if yer that desperate, I cud give yer one o'mine!" And the company roared with laughter again.

Suddenly, a door in the back of the room opened and a lady stood there, a wool shawl over her white nightgown and wrap.

She held up a candle that shone on the gold hair, now threaded with more than a hint of white, peeping out from under a nightcap. Her pretty face was lined with both age and sorrow.

"What is this commotion?" she asked, her quiet voice immediately quelling the laughter.

"Madame, this gentleman is looking for a boy," repeated Joseph.

"Then he has come to the wrong place. There is no boy here," said Claire. Her calm gaze, educated voice and ladylike demeanor did more than anything else to strike doubt into Augustus' heart.

"I... I may have made a mistake, Madame, But I...."

"Yes, you undoubtedly have. I would ask you to leave now. We are on the verge of closing. These gentlemen are leaving."

At her word, the customers began to gather themselves together and stand up.

"But, I was hoping for a meal and a room for the night," said Augustus, "I haven't...."

"I'm sorry. The kitchen is long since closed and the taps are off the barrels. And all our rooms are taken. You need to bespeak one in advance next time. You were lucky to find us open at all."

The men stumbled into the street, laughing and repeating *looking fer a boy*; *don't rightly know 'is name*; *y'can 'ave one o' mine*. Augustus was forced to follow them, and heard the door being bolted behind him. He stood for a moment, looking up at the creaking sign, before giving a sigh and turning back to the carriage. The driver was all but asleep and the horses' heads hung down to the ground, but their ordeal was not yet over.

Augustus directed them to his uncle's house in Brede. The way was pitch dark and the country lanes confusing. Branches caught at the carriage on both sides as it lumbered up narrow paths, barely wider than the vehicle. The six or seven miles took them over an hour. When they arrived, the house was in darkness. Augustus hammered on the door until at last the housekeeper appeared, a shawl thrown over her nightwear.

"Mr. Augustus!" she cried. "We weren't expecting you!"

"You mean you never got my letter?" lied the visitor. "I tell you, the mail is becoming increasingly unreliable! Well, you'll just have to make up a bed and tell old Munter to rustle something up. I... er, expected to be earlier and I haven't dined. I'm starving."

Suddenly, a shot rang out from the darkness beyond just what Augustus knew to be the confines of his uncle's property. The horses had again been standing with their heads low, but they startled and reared up. The driver had all he could do to hold them. Augustus pushed the housekeeper out of the way and ran inside, oblivious to the driver and horses behind him.

"It's only Squire Collingswood," said the housekeeper, thinking what a poor excuse for a man Augustus was, with no thought for anyone but himself. "He's shooting at poachers. How he can see them in this dark is beyond me, but he's been out there every night this week."

She went down the steps and pointed the driver to the stables, telling him to come in by the kitchen door afterwards, and she'd find a mouthful of something for him. "Don't go walking around with that fool next door shooting at anything that moves," she said. "It doesn't look like any of us can expect any help from dear Augustus!"

Neither she nor Munter was fond of their employer's nephew. He'd never been known to give them any sort of a *douceur* when he stayed there and did nothing but cause them more work.

"Don't I know it!" said the driver, and clicked up the poor horses one last time.

A few minutes later, Augustus was in the drawing room where he'd kicked the fire into flame and put on another log. He was helping himself to a generous slug of his uncle's sherry. The housekeeper came in with a plate of bread and cheese.

"I'm sorry, sir. I can't rouse Munter. He's a fearful deep sleeper. This is all I can find." She didn't say there had been a nice piece of ham pie in the larder, but she'd given it to the driver. And she didn't put a warm brick in their guest's bed. She may not have thought of it in those terms, but at heart she was a supporter of the ideals of the French Revolution: Liberty, Equality, Fraternity. Bernard Rambuteau would have approved.

Chapter Thirty-Four

London 1816

Phillipa's father, the Reverend Philip Warner, was a tall, handsome gentleman in his sixties. He had the stern profile of a Greek statue, a noble nose and square chin. It was easy to imagine him above his flock in the pulpit, exhorting them to adhere to the straight and narrow path. His own path appeared relatively soft underfoot, as he had a generously wealthy parish and a subservient wife. He only had to look around for her to be by his side, a small, thin woman with a worried crease between her eyes, asking anxiously if he needed something.

Philippa was the daughter of their old age, and having been brought up by the one to revere the other, and the other to ignore the first, she listened intently to what her father had to say, and barely noticed her mother. Rory could at once see it was from her father she had not only her name, her good looks, and her high moral rectitude, but also the ability to ignore anything or anyone she felt beneath her.

He was welcomed with great solemnity and invited to partake in a light nuncheon, of which the Reverend partook anything but lightly, and Philippa's mother ate nearly nothing, concerned only that everything should be to their guest's liking. Rory tried to engage them all in inconsequential chatter about the beauties of the autumn foliage, the fine weather they had so far enjoyed, and the novelties now appearing on the London stage.

But when the Reverend declared that the only time he had seen Kean at the Drury Lane Theatre he had found the actor's grimacing entirely unconvincing, and Philippa announced that she had heard of the hippodromes at Astley's Theatre, but anything of that nature, with men performing ridiculous stunts with beasts, was anathema to her, he gave up. He spent his time planning how he would induce her father to refuse his suit. That was the only way he could think of to put an end to the proposed betrothal, which was now figuring in his mind as an entry into Hades.

He reckoned, however without the worthy Reverend's attachment to the idea of his daughter being the wife of a Peer. When at last the ghastly meal was over and he was led into his host's study, he realized he was lost. "Come now, my lord," said Philippa's father, smiling genially when Rory described his attachment to wine with dinner and port after it, "what you describe is a natural addiction to intoxicants, that with time and the encouragement of her future ladyship, you will surely overcome."

And when Rory described the sporting engagements he enjoyed, including betting on any and all horseraces, and the recent (entirely fictitious) backing of a friend in a wager he would wear his clothing inside out and walk backwards down Pall Mall, the rector merely laughed with apparent great good humor. "Tush, now, we need not tell the ladies my dear sir," he said smugly, glancing in the direction of the drawing room where his wife and daughter awaited the outcome of the interview, "but we all of us enjoy a harmless flutter now and then."

Finally, the reluctant suitor was driven to explain to his potential father-in-law that, though his daughter would be treated with every courtesy and affection due his wife, there was no denying that Lord Dexter had a roving eye. Even this was met with complaisance. "Between us, my lord," said the righteous man with a look of masculine understanding, "the attractions of one's helpmeet do, let us say, pall in time. It is a very strong man who can withstand the lure of another lady, should she show herself willing."

After this, Rory gave up. If the Reverend was prepared to countenance drinking, gambling and marital infidelity in his daughter's spouse, there was nothing he could say that would prevent his approval of the betrothal. Finally, in desperation, Rory claimed an engagement he had only just remembered, he made his excuses to his hosts, placed his now officially betrothed's hand under his arm, and led her to the carriage for home. He was silent all the way back to London. Philippa appeared not to notice, her head bent over Fordyce's sermons until it became too dark to read. The weather seemed at one with his mood. It had come on to rain.

It was nearly nine by the time he deposited his companion at her aunt's home and arrived at his own front door. His heavy, despairing tread in the hall brought the butler from his *loge*. After taking his master's hat and cloak, he brought him the note lying on the console table.

"From Mrs. Ramsay, sir," he said. "I draw your attention to her note, late as it is, because her man indicated it was of some urgency."

Rory tore open the envelope and devoured the contents. His did not hesitate for a moment. He turned around and told the butler to send his valet up immediately, and to have his big grey saddled at once. He was leaving in ten minutes. He bounded up the stairs two at a time and was pulling off his superfine fitted coat even before his valet arrived. "Riding coat and boots, and a bag with a change of linen," he said shortly. He was downstairs again in under ten minutes, shrugging on his heavy, caped riding cloak with its capacious pockets.

He went into his study and unlocked a drawer in his desk, taking out a mahogany box which, when opened, revealed a pair of dueling pistols. He took them out, one by one, and hefted them. They were a fine, balanced pair made by Manton that had belonged to his father. He used them regularly in practice and was a good shot, so he'd only been forced to use them seriously once before.

He had been challenged by a man who found him *in flagrante* with his wife. He had deloped, firing over his head, thinking it would be dishonorable to even try to kill a man he had cuckolded. Fortunately, his opponent had been a very poor shot and his bullet had come nowhere near. Nevertheless, he'd been much more careful in his choice of female companionship after that.

Now, he took the pistols from the box together with a bag of pre-loaded balls he kept separately in the drawer. He put them in his deep pockets, turned back into the hall, picked up his curly-brimmed beaver and riding gloves, and was out of the house before anyone had a chance to say anything. The big grey was restive as he pulled himself into the saddle and called to the groom to let him go.

It was drizzling with rain, but even at that time of night, the traffic still thronged the London streets. Carriages were conveying party-goers to their destinations, curricles and barouches drove the younger set from dinner to the clubs, and the occasional sedan chair was still in use, carrying a dowager or what the wags would call *a prime article* to their widely different destinations. On top of that, hackneys plied their trade, tradespeople clopped their way home at the end of a busy day, link boys ran along offering their services, flower sellers thrust their last posies through the windows of carriages, and the occasional drunk wandered into the road to be sworn at by everyone.

Rory threaded his way expertly through all of it, going east until he could see the London Bridge. As a boy he had learned from his tutor, who was something of an expert in London history, that the bridge used to have a row of shops, and even public latrines across its length. He had found out later there were brothels, too, but naturally his tutor hadn't mentioned those. By the 1770's these had all finally been either destroyed by accidental fire or removed, and he had heard that now that the ancient bridge itself was going to be replaced.

But as the traffic thinned, Rory thought of none of this. He was thinking about Héloise's note. She had a son, and Augustus Protheroe was his father. She had become a courtesan to pay for her son's education. Now it all made sense, except for why she had refused him. He understood why she was desperate to keep the boy from Protheroe. He was a man Rory had never trusted, instinctively knowing he was a poltroon.

Chapter Thirty-Five

Hastings 1816

The little family at the Traveller's Rest exclaimed with joy when they saw Héloise, but it wasn't until the horses had been stabled, Alf had been fed and given a room for the night, and she had been in to see her peacefully sleeping son, that she explained the reason for the unexpected visit.

"Just let him try to come here and take Emile," growled Joseph. "He'll have to do it over my dead body."

"Dear Joseph!" said Héloise, hugging him. "That's just it, I don't want any dead bodies. And Augustus has the right to take him, I'm sorry to say. But I'm hoping if I can simply hide us both, he'll give up and go away. I'm afraid I'll have to give up the rest of my plans of making money for Emile's education and our future in England, and really disappear. Perhaps we should all go back to France. I have twenty thousand pounds. That should get us somewhere."

"Twenty thousand pounds!" exclaimed Agnès. "You never earned all that as a governess!"

So the truth about Héloise's occupation had to come out. Agnès and Joseph were round-eyed and incredulous, first that their dear Héloise would countenance such a profession, but then it must be said, that she could command such a price.

"Five thousand for three months!" exclaimed Agnès. "Those men must have more money than sense!" She realized what she had said and laughed. "I mean, we all think you're priceless, Mademoiselle, but that's more than fifty pounds a day for... well, you know!"

"People only value you at what you value yourself," said Héloise, laughing in spite of herself at Agnès's scandalized expression. And I can tell you I was once offered double."

"Double?" they all cried. "Did you take it?"

"No, I... I didn't like him at all."

How could she explain she had liked the man only too well? That in fact, she would have taken him for nothing. But those were deep waters and she would not wade in. So she changed the subject by saying, "I did ask a... a friend to help me if he could, but, well, I don't suppose he will come. We need to make plans of our own."

They talked over the situation for another hour, deciding that France might, after all, be the best option. Strangely, none of those who had left that country over twenty years before had any real desire to go back. They might like to visit, to see family and old friends, but their life was now here, at the inn they had poured their work and faith into. Claire could not bear the idea of leaving her husband's grave. She still visited it every day. Only with him could she could talk about their daughter. Besides, the channel crossing was still a dreadful memory none of them wanted to repeat. But for the sake of Héloise and Emile, they would go, not back to Paris, but to Bordeaux.

That night, Héloise slept at the inn, but the following morning she walked over to the vicarage to have a very difficult conversation with Alice and Julian Beresford. Their reaction was much more muted than that of Agnès and Joseph, but even more shocked. The idea that their goddaughter should have taken to prostitution, for that's the unvarnished truth of what it was, was almost more than they could take in.

"I know I shouldn't ask you to shelter someone who is living a life that is the opposite to everything you stand for," she said, "but I have nowhere else to go."

"Our good Lord himself didn't turn away the woman taken in prostitution," said Julian Beresford slowly, "And who are we to do less than he? Of course you may come here. We shall be glad to have you and Emile. It will be quite like old times."

For they both had fond memories of a long-limbed young woman whose plaits were constantly unravelling, running around the house with their boys. So it was, that when Augustus arrived at the inn that night, Joseph could say truthfully that neither Héloise nor her son were there. He had offered free drinks to anyone who would stay until the expected visitor arrived and disclaim all knowledge of "the boy".

Everyone knew the subterfuge could only last so long. Emile was well known in their end of the town, since he ran with a pack of lads his age whenever he was freed from his lessons. He was considered one of them. He spoke like the locals and was a cheerful, high-spirited boy, always ready for a dare. He had his mother's wide grey eyes and chestnut curls, and was a particular favorite with the local women. They were charmed when he recited one of the French poems his grandmother had taught him, and then turned around and talked to his friends in the broadest Sussex dialect.

Emile's bedroom in the vicarage had belonged to one of the twins, and was full of their old toys. It faced east and the early morning light shining in his eyes woke him. He got up and for a while played with the lead soldiers that had always fascinated Sebastian. In fact, his desire to go into the army was born from playing with those very soldiers. Then Emile built a few forts with the blocks and made the soldiers fall to their doom from the highest places. By now he was hungry and wandered down to the kitchen where Mary, the maid, was putting up the morning tea trays.

"Hello young Aymeel," she said, "I didn't know you was here. Want some sugar-bread?"

"Yes, please!" said the young man, whose manners were always perfect, even when his speech wasn't. "That I would!"

The maid cut him a large slice of bread and liberally sprinkled it with sugar, poured him a glass of milk and left him to it, while she took up the tea-trays. When she got back down, he had finished and was rubbing his sticky hands on his nightgown.

"I'll bring up some warm water and do you wash yersel'," she said. "Then my Archie says as he were a-goin' to c'llect conkers this mornin'. You want t' go along a him and get yersel' some."

Mary's Archie was one of the lads who always knew where the best conkers, or horse chestnuts, were to be found in the autumn, the best tadpoles in the spring, and the best wild strawberries in the summer. He was a year or so older than Emile, and one of his heroes. It didn't take a second bidding for the boy to get dressed, pull on his boots and coat and run outside before anyone in the house saw him.

He had just begun to take lessons with the vicar and was finding it hard going. If his teacher didn't see him, perhaps he'd forget he was supposed to copy out that passage from Tacitus' *Agricola* that had to do with the superiority of the liberty amongst the Britons compared with the Romans. Who cared about liberty when there were conkers to be had?

He ran to Mary's cottage and was in time to see Archie emerge with a doorstep-sized chunk of bread covered with a thick layer of dripping, the solidified fat from the Sunday roast. Delicious.

"You want some?" offered Archie. Emile nodded and took a big bite. Chewing companionably, they walked along, meeting up with a couple of other boys bent on the same mission. They kicked stones and threw sticks at the neighborhood cats (none of which met its mark) until the housewives shouted at them to "Give over! I know oo yer mothers are!"

Then they disappeared into the woods at the bottom of the old cemetery, where huge old horse chestnut trees stood. The trick was not necessarily to find the biggest chestnuts, but the toughest, so the boys scuffed amongst the fallen shiny brown knobs, some still encased in their hard, prickly skins, picking up pocketfuls of likely candidates. Then they went into the graveyard, and ignoring the antiquity or importance of the tombstones that lay fallen in the grass, used them as tables on which they placed the chestnuts to hammer slim nails through the center. Then they ran string though the holes, tied them off at the bottom and challenged each other.

The trick was to hit your opponent's conker and shatter it. It was a foul if you hit his fingers; he would get two chances to smash your weapon. But there were always challenges. "Yer moved yer 'and!" "Yer string's too long," (the dimensions were supposed to be exact), "Yer coward! Yer stepped back!" This often led to loud disagreements and often fisticuffs, but by the time it was deemed to be getting on for the dinner hour, Emile held the winning conker. It was a seven-er, which meant it had smashed seven opponents.

They had started back down the street towards Archie's (for Emile was still disinclined to go to the vicarage and face Tacitus), when a big old carriage came towards them. The boys were strung out over the road and the driver sounded a klaxon that forced them to jump to one side as it trotted past. Emile caught the gaze of the passenger who stared at the him and called for the driver to halt. The group of boys was astonished to see a gentleman jump out, grab Emile by the collar and bundle him into the carriage.

Chapter Thirty-Six

Hastings 1816

Rory Compton urged his big horse into a canter across the Thames and, like Augustus several hours before him, set his head for Sevenoaks in Kent, a place he knew a little. Not many were aware that amongst his charities, Lord Dexter supported the education of boys whose parents could not afford the more famous schools, such as the one he himself had gone to. He had visited the Queen Elizabeth School in Sevenoaks at the invitation of the Headmaster. He knew it was about thirty miles from London and almost half way to Hastings. He would find an inn in the town, rest himself and his horse, then be up early to arrive in Hastings before a man like Protheroe would be out of bed.

It was a chilly night with a continuous drizzle. His heavy cloak kept most of it off, but it was an uncomfortable ride and he was glad when he came into the town. He had had no difficulty seeing the lanterns of the inns, which surprised him by appearing to be doing a bang-up trade. Then he found out about the cattle market. By now the farmers had eaten and drunk their fill, but, as usual, a number of them had been unable to make their way home and were now snoring in the rooms upstairs. "Sorry, all full, not a bed to be had for love or money," was the refrain wherever he went. He was forced to ride on, chilled, damp, and hungry.

"Dammit, he said to himself, what was that poem whatever-her-name-was read to me that time? Oh yes, *Young Lochinvar*. He remembered it now.

So faithful in love, and so dauntless in war
There never was knight like the young Lochinvar!

I bet he never had to put up with this!" He laughed ironically to himself. "So much for Romance!"

He considered going to the school and asking for a bed, but didn't relish explaining what he was doing riding to Hastings in the middle of the night. So he buried his chin into his cloak collar and rode on in the rain.

A couple of miles out of Sevenoaks he passed through a village in the center of which a mean-looking dwelling had a creaking sign hanging in front. It was an inn of some sort. Well, beggars couldn't be choosers. He banged on the door until a disreputable looking woman opened it. She looked the visitor up and down and apparently decided he was worth the aggravation.

"Good evening, Madam," he said politely. "I need a room for the night and stabling for my horse."

"No good madam-ing me" she replied sourly. "It'll cost yer ten guineas either way, extra for the 'orse."

Ten guineas was more than double what a reputable inn might have cost.

"Four guineas, horse included," he countered.

"Five, extra for the 'orse."

"Five all in."

"Done."

She spat on her hand and extended it. Luckily, he was still wearing his riding gloves, so he took it.

"Take yer nag around the back, yer Honor," said his hostess, suddenly accommodating. "The lad'll see to 'im. He's a bit simple, but you tell 'im plain wot yer wants and 'e'll do it. You'll be wanting a bite t' eat, I shouldn't wonder."

"Well...," said Rory, "if it's not too much trouble." He wondered what on earth a place like this might offer in the way of dinner. But he was cold and wet. Anything warm would do.

Lord Dexter led his horse to the stable and roused the boy, who shambled forward, his stiff hair the color and texture of the straw he was standing in. His eyes slid away from Rory, to the horse.

"Thass a big 'orse," he pronounced.

"Yes. His name is Jupiter. He needs a drink, then well rubbing down, and hay and straw for his bedding. Can you do that?"

"Yuss. Rub 'im down, give 'im 'is dinner and straw."

"Exactly. I'll come back in a while and if you've done it all, I'll give you this." He produced a silver coin from his pocket and showed it to the boy, who made a grab for it.

"You'll get it when I see you've done what I said. Now, let me see you take off his harness."

Rory stood while the lad took the reins and led the big horse into the stable. He seemed to know what he was doing, taking the harness off, pumping some water into a pail, and gathering handfuls of straw to begin the rubdown, all the while talking to the animal in some language of his own. Jupiter nickered in his ear in a way Rory knew meant he was content. He wondered if he was going to be so lucky himself.

A few hours later, he knew he wasn't. The landlady had offered him a watery soup, in which floated a bit of what looked and smelled like mutton gristle, a piece of carrot and half an onion. He had eaten the carrot and left the gristle and onion. Then he drank the almost tasteless broth which was, at least, hot. He'd put his wet cloak and hat back on to go and check on Jupiter, and found him perfectly happy in a dry stall, pulling at a pile of fresh hay in the corner. The boy was watching him, hanging over the half-gate.

"E's a nice 'orse," said the lad. I give 'im 'alf me apple I was saving. "E dint 'alf like it!"

"Yes, he is," agreed Rory, "and thank you for the apple."

He gave the silver sixpence to the boy, who bit it between a set of very dirty teeth and smiled broadly before secreting it somewhere inside his filthy coat. Rory was glad at least he didn't have to worry about his horse.

Then he went back into the inn and climbed up to his bedchamber. There was no fire, indeed, no fireplace, and it was freezing cold. He took off his cloak and hat and then his britches and coat, and got into the bed. The sheets were icy. As his body heat warmed them slightly, he realized they were also damp. This was not surprising, as the windows rattled in their frames and the rain, now coming down in earnest, was forming a puddle on the floor. He got up again, put his britches and jacket back on, threw his heavy cloak over the bed, and climbed back in. It was slightly better, but not much. He slept fitfully, waking with the cold morning air and conscious of a tickle at the back of his throat.

The sky had only begun to lighten and it was not yet dawn but he got up. His calls for the landlady went unanswered, so he finally went down to the kitchen and found a pan of warmish water over the embers of the fire. He used a sliver of carbolic soap he found next to a collection of rags and shaved by touch, since he had no mirror. He went back upstairs, undressed, shivering, and put on the clean linen his valet had packed in his bag. With no mirror, he could not see his attempt to tie a fresh neckcloth, but it would have to do. He put his crumpled britches and coat back on, pulled on his riding boots, grabbed his cloak and hat, and went downstairs.

He left five coins on the table, thinking it was the worst money he'd ever spent, and went out to the stable. It had stopped raining, thank God, though there was a chill wind. The boy was sleeping in a pile of straw outside the big horse's stall. Rory wondered how he wasn't frozen, but the lad jumped up at Rory's approach and didn't seem even slightly surprised at his pre-dawn departure. The sun was only just beginning to appear over the horizon when Lord Dexter began what proved to be a four-hour ride to Hastings, the wind in his face and the tickle at the back of his throat becoming more and more pronounced.

Chapter Thirty-Seven

Hastings 1816

Augustus woke up earlier than he expected the morning after his arrival at his uncle's home, and having rung for coffee, made a leisurely toilette. He had returned to his earlier habits of not eating breakfast, and when he was ready wandered downstairs. His uncle was in the drawing room, as always, looking at his ancient penny.

"Augustus, my boy!" he said. "Ivy told me you were here. We weren't expecting you, but I expect you felt you needed a break. Been damned hard for you, I imagine, losing your wife like that."

His nephew assumed the desolated expression he always adopted when Mildred was mentioned. "Yes, it's been a trial. Had to leave the estate after a bit. Needed to get to London, but then, you know, London...."

"No need to tell me, no need to tell me," said his uncle. "I've never been happier than since I came here. Living surrounded by antiquity, knowing yourself one of a line reaching back..., that's the way to feel really alive. Did you know...," and he launched into an explanation of the discovery of the penny he had in his hands, the same explanation Augustus had heard fifty times before.

"Yes, yes, uncle. So you've said. Very interesting." Augustus tried to stem the flood of verbiage that flowed like a never-ending stream from his uncle's lips. He didn't think he could bear to hear another word of it. He made a decision. "I hope you don't mind, but I won't be lunching with you today. Sorry, it being my first day here and all that, but I... I'm expected for lunch in Hastings."

"Ah, Hastings! Now there's a place full of history. Most people know as the place of battle when the Normans invaded in 1066, but the town is much older than that. The settlement was already there when the Romans arrived in Britain for the first time in 55 BC. Why, my penny is evidence of...." And he was off again.

"Yes, of course, well, see you later!" Augustus almost ran from the room. He had decided to go back to *The Traveller's Rest.* The smell of whatever they'd had there yesterday had stayed in his nose for a long time the night before. He knew that Munter's luncheon would be delicious, but if he stayed, he'd have to listen to his uncle. He fancied a peaceful meal. He'd go back there, even if Héloise wasn't there and the boy never existed.

He pulled the bell, but since his uncle had no butler, no one came. In the end, he went down to the kitchen and there found his coachman enjoying a mug of beer and a large slice of roast beef.

"When you've *quite* finished, you can harness up the horses and bring round the carriage," snapped Augustus, "I'm going back into Hastings."

The drive was considerably easier this morning than it had been in the dark the night before, and it wasn't too long before they were clopping down the London Road that led out of Hastings.

Suddenly, the driver sounded the horn and shouted, "Get out o' the way, yer varmints!"

Augustus looked out of the window and saw a group of scruffy boys walking down the middle of the road. One of them turned and he saw the unmistakable face of Héloise. It was a dirty version to be sure, but with those wide eyes, white skin, and curls, it had to be her son.

"Stop! Stop the carriage!" shouted Augustus and hammered on the roof with the head of his cane.

No sooner were the horses reined in than Augustus jumped from the carriage, ran back and took the boy by his dirty collar. He half carried, half walked him back to the carriage, shut the door and banged on the roof for the driver to continue. "Put 'em along, you idiot!" he yelled.

The horses picked up speed so that the boys who were running behind were soon out of sight round a bend in the road. Emile, for it was of course he, was not the sort of boy to submit to such treatment. He suddenly remembered the words of Tacitus concerning Britons and Liberty. He took his prize conker out of his pocket and, drawing his arm back as far as he could in the confines of the carriage, hammered his captor hard on the knee. It was evidence of the ferocity of the blow that the conker shattered. It would never be an eight-er.

Tears of pain starting to his eyes, Augustus screamed and, dropping his stick, grabbed his knee with both hands. Emile didn't stay to mourn the loss of his conker. Copying his captor's actions, he picked up the cane and rapped hard on the ceiling of the carriage, shouting *Stop*!

Before the carriage even came to a halt, Emile had the door open and was in the road. He knew where he was. He was close to *The Traveller's Rest*, on the outskirts of the town. He ran there as fast as he could, threw himself through the front door and ran through the saloon into the kitchen, where he saw his mother and grandmother, both in tears.

"Emile! Where have you been? I was so worried about you!" cried his mother, speaking to him, as she always did, in French.

"I went collecting conkers with Archie. Then a man pulled me into his carriage but I hit him on the knee with my seven-er and jumped out. Broke my conker." Emile larded his response with English, since *conkers* and *seven-ers* had no French equivalent, as far as he knew.

There was a commotion in the saloon, and a cry of "Where is he? By God, the whelp's got spirit! Where's my son?"

They all rushed into the front room, and there beheld Augustus, leaning on his stick, a broad smile on his face.

Chapter Thirty-Eight

Hastings 1816

Because of his early start, it was still not more than eleven in the morning when Lord Dexter rode into Hastings. In a croak, for his throat was now very sore, he asked a woman returning from the bakery with a loaf of bread under her arm the way to *The Traveller's Rest*. Because it enjoyed a certain fame, she was able to tell him. The smell of the fresh bread smote his nostrils and he almost asked the way to the bakery, for he had eaten nothing except the watery soup at the inn since lunching with the Reverend the day before.

He smiled wryly at the memory of that visit, and wondered what his betrothed would say if she saw him now, on a wild goose chase at the request of a woman she would certainly not acknowledge. He was poorly-shaven, ill-kempt, and he now realized as a flush went through him, feverish with a damned cold. But he simply thanked his informant and continued on his way.

He walked his weary horse, feeling worse and worse himself, wondering what he was doing there. Why had he come? Protheroe had a right to the child after all. A father's rights were pre-eminent in law. *A father's rights*....

His thoughts were interrupted as he came upon a group of boys running furiously down the road. Running himself, he caught up with them and asked what the problem was. It wasn't easy to get an answer with everyone running, but he finally understood:

"It's Emile. That man in the coach's got 'im. We're goin' to rescue 'im."

As they rounded the bend, they saw the heavy old coach drawn up outside *The Traveller's Rest*.

Lord Dexter threw open the inn door and entered the saloon, surrounded by a group of panting boys. "Where's Emile?" he croaked to an astonished company. Augustus Protheroe, had hobbled towards the back of the room where Héloise and Claire gathered the boy into their skirts. "I've come to see my son."

There was complete silence.

"*Your* son?" said Augustus when he could gather his wits.

"Certainly." Rory mopped his burning forehead with his handkerchief and tried to speak more clearly. "He has been staying here with his, er... godmother," he bowed towards Claire, "learning French. He will soon be leaving for Eton. He has a place there."

"There's something wrong with you, Dexter," blustered Augustus, "anyone can see that. The boy is *my* son. I am here to take him away."

"Be so kind as to tell me *the boy's* name, then, Protheroe."

Augustus, who still didn't know Emile's name, was aware that it had been spoken, but Lord Dexter's voice was so hoarse that he hadn't quite caught it.

"Edmund," he pronounced. "My son's name is Edmund."

"In that case, the boy here is certainly not he. This child's name is Emile, as I well know because I chose it, in honor of his French heritage." Rory's chest heaved. He mopped his face again and croaked, "Come here, Emile, and greet your father."

Emile, though not bookish, was far from stupid. In an instant he sized up the two men who were claiming to be his father, an individual he had always believed was dead, and decided which one he preferred. He walked quickly over to Lord Dexter and held out his hand.

"I'm glad to see you again, Father," he said, in his best Mayfair English.

"This is nonsense!" roared Augustus. "The boy is mine. I had a... liaison with his mother in September of 1808. When is your birthday, boy?"

"In June," replied Emile.

"There, what did I tell you?" Augustus gave an ugly smile. Nine months after I was here."

"But I was here in September of 1808, too," said Rory, his chest heaving with the effort of speaking. "Easy to remember. There were rumors about how...," he stopped and took a breath, "... how the Russians were going to react to B... Bonaparte's treaty with the P... Prussians. I was on my way to a quick trip to... Paris." Rory had to clear his throat again. "I... er, comforted H... Héloïse after the departure of the man who had taken advantage of her. You, I suppose, Protheroe."

"Nice behavior indeed, for a young woman!" spat Augustus. "It seems either one of us could be the boy's father." He looked at Emile, standing next to Rory. "He has nothing of you in him, as far as one can see. Though at the moment you look sick as a dog."

"Nor... of you... either," came the breathless reply. "He's the image of his... mother." Lord Dexter smiled at Héloise, who had been listening to all this, dumbfounded. He mopped his face again. "Settle this the... the gentlemanly way, Protheroe. Duel. Winner claims the boy."

"A duel? Impossible. I have neither sword nor pistols with me."

"Not swords, too old-fashioned." Lord Dexter was finding it increasingly hard to catch his breath. "H... happen to have my pistols with me. Roads so unsafe you know. H... here, you choose."

Rory withdrew a pistol from each pocket and lay them on the table. He mopped his face. He looked awful.

Héloise started towards him, "A duel? No! Lord Dexter, no! You cannot! Anyway, you're in no state to...."

He held up his hand. "Settle this now," he said. "It's best this way."

Augustus picked up each of the pistols in turn and considered. His knee was giving him a good deal of pain, and he could cry off on that account, but Dexter was obviously not well. He was feverish and couldn't breathe. His eyes seemed unfocussed. This might be the moment to get rid of him once and for all. The Ramsay woman, or whatever her name was, and her son would both be his. The opportunity seemed too good to miss.

"Very well, Dexter," he said. He picked up each of the pistols in turn. They were identical. "Not but this isn't very irregular. We have no seconds, no doctor...."

"I can act as a doctor," said Claire, coming forward calmly, and Joseph here will act as your second. If Lord Dexter pleases, the carriage driver Alf will second him."

Alf, who had driven Héloise down from London the day before was so enjoying the good food and comfortable bed at *The Traveller's Rest* that he had stayed on a second night.

Rory nodded his agreement, and Protheroe was forced to do the same.

So it was that two English gentlemen, members of the *ton*, went out into the orchard at the back of an inn in a small country town to face each other in a duel attended by a barman, the driver of a hired carriage, an excited group of boys too young to shave, and three French women.

The fruit had by now been gathered from the trees, and in the recent wind and rain, the branches had shed most of their leaves. But Joseph kept the wide rows between the apple trees scrupulously clear and it made a perfectly acceptable space for a duel. The women tried to shoo the boys away, especially Emile, but they scattered in all directions and then gradually returned, taking up positions behind the trees, their eyes drinking in every aspect of the best excitement they had ever had. It even beat the pugilistic bouts that took place at the summer fair when the aptly named Hercules took on all comers. They were always sure of blood, but they'd never witnessed actual death.

As the one who had been challenged, Augustus had the right to choose the distance and the first of the weapons. They were loaded by the seconds and indistinguishable from each other. The opponents removed their hats, cloaks and white neckcloths. Both were glad to be wearing dark coats with no shining buttons. Rory warned that the pistols had a hair trigger, and the opponents held their weapons down while the seconds, back to back, each paced off fifteen feet and established the position from which the shots would be fired.

The women huddled together at a safe distance, the seconds flipped a coin to see who should drop the white handkerchief signal to shoot, and all was ready. Lord Dexter turned sideways and looked down the barrel of his weapon. He was alternately shivering and sweating, but by sheer force of will he held the pistol steady.

It was at this point that Augustus realized he had made a mistake. His knee was aching abominably and he could hardly stand straight. He could see his opponent's steady weapon and firm gaze: though his face was a ghastly color, he suddenly did not look ill at all. All at once, Augustus knew he couldn't do it. He gave a great cry, threw his pistol to the ground where it fired into the turf, and hobbled off as fast as his injured knee would allow.

The big old carriage was still waiting, the driver dozing inside, the slab of beef and mug of beer having induced a comfortable somnolence. He had not seen the whole company go out into the orchard at the back of the building, and only awoke when Augustus yelled at him to make haste. He scrambled onto the box, whipped up the unfortunate horses and made for Brede with as much speed as he and they could muster .

The astonishment at Protheroe's behavior was quickly replaced by consternation as Lord Dexter crumpled and fell where he stood. Everyone thought he had been hit by the bullet discharged by his opponent's weapon. Héloise screamed "Rory!" and ran to him. Joseph picked up the pistol dropped by Augustus and saw where the bullet had entered the earth. Alf and the two other women did their best to keep the children back from the scene, while Joseph carefully retrieved the other weapon from Rory's limp hand. Feeling himself about to faint, Rory had snicked on the safety catch.

It was soon apparent he was neither dead nor wounded, but suffering from a collapse brought on by his feverish cold, an exhausting ride, and the fact he had neither eaten nor drunk anything but a bowl of watery soup in almost twenty-four hours.

Chapter Thirty-Nine

Hastings 1816

Augustus sank back against the squabs of the big old carriage, huddled in the heavy horsehair blanket, miserable for a variety of reasons. He had left behind his cloak, neckcloth, hat and cane and he was cold. The pain in his knee was abominable. But most of all, he knew his reputation was done for. He had run away from a duel, something no gentleman should in honor do. Dexter and the Ramsay woman would surely spread it around; London would be impossible. Until his knee healed, he would have to rusticate here in the country with his uncle and his damned penny. Then he could go abroad until the noise died down.

And none of it was his fault! Why had he been forced to fight a duel for something that was his by right? Dexter and the woman were lying, of course, just as everyone lied to him. Those servants of hers had lied when they said they didn't know where she was. Mildred had lied when she'd married him. She hadn't wanted a husband, just a dogsbody to do her bidding. He passed his life in review, dwelling on all the rotten luck that had befallen him. Bad luck at every turn, that's what his whole life had been.

By the time he arrived at his uncle's home, he was full of self-pity, disgusted with everything and everyone, and hungry, for he'd had nothing to eat since the bread and cheese the night before. He hobbled into the house to find it quiet. His uncle was, he supposed, in his study, poring over the ancient maps and manuscripts he kept there. As usual, no one came in answer to the bell, and he was forced to roar down the kitchen stairs for someone to damned well bring him something to eat and make a poultice for his knee.

Ivy, the housekeeper, arrived finally with a bowl of soup left over from luncheon and a sandwich made from the few scraps of beef that remained. Munter was taking his afternoon nap, which meant he was lying on his bed with the rest of the lunchtime bottle of wine, and had no intention of moving. She exclaimed at his knee, which she could see was swollen from the way it puffed out under his close-fitting pantaloons.

"We'll have to cut them up the side to get at that knee," she said. "however did you come to injure it like that?"

He wasn't about to tell her he'd been hit by an seven-year-old boy with a conker, so he made up some story about one of the horses kicking him.

"Well, I don't rightly know what to do for it. If you was a horse, I suppose we'd put a hot bran plaster on it. I could give that a try."

I'm not having any hot bran on my knee, thank you very much. Wrap it up with some warm cloths, that should do it."

While the housekeeper was getting the bandages, he drank the soup and ate the sandwich. There was no wine, of course. His uncle kept his fine collection under lock and key and he wasn't going approach him, for fear of another history lecture. But there was a nearly new bottle of brandy on the side table because the old fool like a snifter before bed. Augustus hobbled over and got it. He couldn't see a glass. No problem. He'd drink it out of the bottle. It was probably contraband, anyway. Everyone knew nobody around here bought brandy that had any tax paid on it.

Ivy returned with a warm cloth, at least it was so hot it made Augustus yelp when she slapped it on his knee, but when it was bound up with a tight bandage, it did begin to feel a bit better. He sat there, his leg up on a stool, drinking the brandy and feeling increasingly morose until it began to get dark. His uncle finally came in and asked him why he hadn't lit any of the candles. He saw the bandaged knee and cut pantaloons and laughed.

"That'll teach you, my boy, to wear your fancy town rig in the country. If you'd had on britches like a sensible man, you wouldn't have had to cut them. Anyway," he carried on, as if Augustus's knee was a thing of no consequence, "I've been looking at some old maps of where they believe Saxon settlements used to be and I've come to the conclusion there's probably one not more than a mile away, down by the stream, you know. Apparently it used to be a bigger river, and the Saxons, of course, would have settled near water. And if you look at my penny, you'll see there's a mark that may or may not indicate a river… I'll just get it and show you…."

Augustus was by now so drunk he'd lost all sense of reality.

"No! Not that bloody penny again!" he shouted. "I can't stand it!" and leaped to his feet. At least, he would have leaped, if his knee had let him. As it was, the minute he put his foot down, a bolt of pain shot down his leg, he staggered and fell into his uncle, who turned, open-mouthed at Augustus's words, from the display case where his ancient penny was kept. He grasped for support at his uncle's hand, and found himself in possession of the infamous coin.

"This damned penny," he yelled, "I know what I'd like to do with it. It came from the ground and by God, it's going back there!"

In spite of his uncle's protestations, and oblivious to his knee, he ran to the front door, wrenched it open and more or less tumbled outside.

The land immediately in front of the house belonged to the property and was kept cut back. There was a number of large rhododendron bushes that grew almost wild in that part of the country and made a nice show in the spring. The neighbor's estate began at the bottom of the garden, not more than fifty feet away. Though tailored for the neighbor's coverts, it was thickly wooded.

Augustus made for the trees and stumbled in, muttering, "Dust to dust, ashes to ashes, it's going back to the land where it came from."

He tripped over a root and almost fell, but instinctively grasped a branch to keep himself off his knee. In so doing he dropped the penny, and then stayed bent double, feeling around trying to find it.

The squire, who had been waiting for poachers every evening that week, was alerted by the sound of someone moving around in his woods. Then he saw the figure bend as if to hide. He lifted his gun and fired. Augustus was right when he said he'd never had any luck. He had just lifted his chest from its bent position, unable to find the penny in the dusk, when the bullet hit him square in the heart. He died on the spot.

It is never pleasant to report that a human being should pass unmourned, but in the case of Augustus, this was, sadly, the case. No one shed a tear. The squire, who was the local magistrate, apologized for the accident and sent a nice wreath to the funeral, but otherwise suffered no consequence of his action. The man had, after all, been on his land. Augustus's uncle was more concerned with the recovery of his penny than his nephew's death. It was found the next morning, bathed in Augustus's blood. He had fallen on it. His valet only mourned the fact that his master had died without making the smallest provision for him after his many years of service.

The family at *The Traveller's Rest* found out about his demise when Joseph returned his cloak, hat and cane left at the scene of the duel. The uncle's direction was in the cloak pocket. The property and fortune of which he was possessed at the time of his death went to a distant second cousin, whom he had never known and who was delighted. The driver of the big old carriage fell in with Alf and together they set up a little carriage-hire business. No one missed it, or the horses.

Chapter Forty

Hastings 1816

Lord Dexter was carried up to the best guest chamber by Joseph and Agnès. They stripped off his damp clothing, put him in a flannel nightshirt and put him in a clean, dry bed with a hot brick at his feet. But in spite of their care and his normal good health, he developed an inflammation of the lungs and a high fever. For two days he tossed and turned, coughing, his breath short and shallow.

When his fever was at its zenith he wheezed odd words Héloise couldn't fathom: *despair or dotage, charming tenderness,* this last accompanied by a breathless chuckle, then something she *did* understand: *got to get there*. Tears came to her eyes and she kissed his hot, damp hand. Claire treated him with cupping and ran her hands over his broad back with the last of the hyssop balm. They took turns sitting by his side, moistening his chapped lips and bathing his temples with cool water.

"What if he doesn't recover, Maman?" said Héloise in despair after forty-eight hours. "It will be my fault. I made him come here in all that bad weather!"

"Nonsense! He's a strong man. I could feel the muscles in his back. Don't worry, he'll recover!"

And of course, he did. The fever broke that afternoon and Dexter fell into a quiet sleep. Her mother urged Héloise to get some rest, but she insisted on staying by the patient's side. They talked quietly about Héloise's life in London, and what she should do now.

Rory became aware of the two women speaking French close to him. It was soothing and he did not open his eyes. Like most aristocrats, Lord Dexter had been brought up to understand that language.

"Why did you refuse him, especially when he offered you double?" Claire was asking.

"I love him, Maman! I knew I couldn't be his mistress for three months and then give him up."

Rory opened his eyes and smiled at the two women, but didn't let them know he had understood.

After that, his recovery was rapid. One day he was sitting up in bed, the next he was sitting at the window, swathed in shawls. The day after, he wanted to get dressed and go downstairs. His nurses protested, but he insisted. Agnès had taken his ill-treated clothing, washed, starched, and ironed what she could, and pressed the rest, commenting on the fine cottons and wools.

Looking more his normal self, he went downstairs and begged writing materials. He needed to tell his mother where he was; he typically went to see her every two or three days, and she would be worried. He doubted anything could assail Philippa's calm, but he thought he should let her know his whereabouts, too. To neither did he say why he had come to Hastings, merely that he was helping a friend.

He wrote to his groom to bring his carriage and pair and collect Jupiter, meekly acquiescing when Claire was adamant she would not permit him to return to London on horseback in the damp and cold. She said she had not used the last of her precious balm to see him fall ill again. Then, until his nemesis discovered him out in the rain and chased him next to the fire, he helped Joseph chop the wood and played with Emile, fencing with sticks in the orchard and being challenged to rowdy games of conkers.

The truth about his French was discovered when Héloise came into the kitchen one day to find him happily conversing with Agnès, picking over blackberries, his long fingers stained purple. She realized he had understood every word she and her mother had said.

"You understand why I kept saying no?" she said.

"Yes, and you had more sense than I. I wouldn't have been able to give you up, either." They looked at each other, the glow of love and understanding in their eyes.

"But I shall sponsor Emile's education," he went on, "so there is no need for you to continue your… working life. I know I have no right to express an opinion, but I wish you would not. You can stay here, or, if you prefer, I will find a house for you and your mother, and your friends," he added, "to live quietly, away from London."

Héloise realized that here was what she had always wanted for her family, why did it now sound so empty?

"And you?" she asked.

"You know I am betrothed to Philippa Warner. I could offer you a *carte blanche* as my mistress, Héloise, but I think it would make us both very unhappy."

They both knew they had no future together. Tears came to Héloise's eyes, and she could not continue the conversation.

A few days later, Lord Dexter reluctantly said the time had come for him to return to London. With Claire's nursing and Agnès's good food he had never felt better in his life. He had seen first-hand the joys of a close and loving family, and his days with Emile had given him a glimpse of fatherhood. But he knew he had to face his responsibilities.

Héloise asked to go back to London with him. "I need to close down my house and make arrangements for my servants," she said, adding with a slight blush, "I know it's not customary for a single lady to travel in a closed carriage such a long way with a gentleman, but, after all, I have no reputation to lose!"

He said nothing, understanding the gulf that separated them.

"You'll have the pleasure of seeing the place where I spent the most miserable night of my life," said Rory lightly, in an attempt to change the subject. Then he laughingly described the appalling dinner and damp bed.

"Jupiter was far better off than I," he smiled. "At least he had an apple!"

"I'm so sorry," said Héloise. "I never imagined...." Her voice tailed off. She could find no words to express her guilty thanks.

"No need to apologize," he said. "It was probably good for me to be uncomfortable for once in my life. It made me see what the majority of the population has to deal with."

They talked about her father and the egalitarian ideals of the French Revolution, now, it seemed, forgotten with the restoration of the monarchy.

"Do you think society will ever enjoy real equality?" wondered Héloise.

"Only when men are happy to have no more than their neighbors, even when they think they deserve more," said Rory. "In my opinion, no, never."

It was a sobering thought.

They overnighted in Sevenoaks, this time avoiding market day and in rooms as far apart from each other as could be managed.

At dinner, they paid no attention to a person in clerical garb dining alone in one corner of the room, but that person, one Edwin Price, certainly noticed Rory Compton, Lord Dexter. He had been until recently a curate in Philippa's father's parish, and knew she had become engaged to his lordship. He had just taken up the very advantageous post of vicar on the estate of a local nobleman. It was his cook's night off and he had come here to dine, preferring to eat the hot meal he knew he could get at the staging post rather than the cold collation left for him at home.

The Reverend Price had had pretentions to Miss Warner's hand himself, and had been pleased when she had not been snapped up in the marriage mart of London. He thought that once he had his own parish, he might have a chance. But then the handsome and eligible Lord Dexter had made his advance.

"Well, well," he said to himself with some satisfaction. "I wonder how dear Philippa would like the idea of her betrothed dining *à deux* with a woman who is most certainly not a relative (for he had made it his business to investigate his opponent's situation in life). And a very good-looking one, at that."

He considered it was certainly his duty to write and tell her.

Chapter Forty-One

London 1816

After his interview with her father, Lord Dexter had driven Philippa back to her aunt's house in a fashionable part of London. It was her aunt who had taken the responsibility for her coming out. Both she and her brother thought Philippa's mother entirely inadequate for the task. Like the Reverend, her aunt was tall, handsome, and very sure of her own worth. Her husband had broken his neck hunting some ten years before and it could not be said that she missed him.

But she was fond of her niece and had been disappointed when her protégée didn't "take". She put it down, rightly, to her rigid behavior. She was overjoyed when Lord Dexter had taken an interest in Philippa.

"My dear," she had said. "They rightly say he who laughs last laughs loudest! You have outshone them all! Rory Compton! I can hardly believe it!"

"Hush, aunt. It is by no means decided," her niece had responded. "I must wait for father's approval. His opinion is paramount."

"But surely, he can have no objections? The man is good-looking, wealthy, and charming. A perfect husband, one would have thought."

"There is, nonetheless, a levity in his character I do not quite like, and I think Papa may feel the same. He is inclined to make a joke of everything."

But, like Rory himself, his daughter underestimated the power of a coronet. The Reverend thought him a fine fellow.

"To be sure, he is inclined, like many of his generation and position, to a certain wildness," he said to his daughter after the interview with her suitor. "But with your firm hand to guide him, I have no doubt he will settle down."

Her mother had liked Lord Dexter very much. He had spoken to her kindly and smilingly thanked her for the excellent nuncheon, a thing no one had done in years. But Philippa cared nothing for her mother's opinion.

When Rory deposited his betrothed and the plain faced duenna back at her aunt's, that lady could scarcely control her impatience.

"Well, what did your father say? He must have been delighted with him!"

"He thought him well enough, though inclined to wildness," answered Philippa, somewhat understating her father's enthusiasm. "He said he'd need a firm hand. I think so too."

She was remembering Rory's comments about Fordyce. She sighed. "I wonder if it is wise for me to marry a man whom I may have to treat more like a child than an equal. He will need a good deal of direction, that much is plain."

244

"But he is so rich and charming! That must count for something!" cried her aunt.

"In the Gospel of Luke," replied Philippa severely, "it plainly says *a man's life consisteth not in the abundance of the things which he possesseth.*"

"Oh, niece! You are too severe! Just think of the gowns, the jewels, the jealously of all the other women!"

But Miss Warner was not convinced. She had been struck by his lordship's response to the Fordyce passage. By nature a cold, passionless person, the idea she would be forced to submit to any sort of uncontrolled emotion made her shudder.

She was quite glad when her fiancé did not put in an appearance for the next few days, and, as he had surmised, was not at all worried. When she received his letter about being with a friend in Hastings, it was, in fact, a relief that she would not be required to sit so close to him any time soon. She passed her days calmly, reading her sermons and sewing the grey dresses she was in the habit of donating to a local orphanage. Grey was such a serviceable color, she always thought.

Rory waited on her the day after his return to the capital from Hastings. He spent a very proper thirty minutes with her and the duenna, whom he had sought to have leave the room, now they were officially engaged. But Philippa demurred.

"There is time for all *that* after we are married," she said.

"All what?" asked Rory, with a smile. "I don't propose to leap on you, you know."

Philippa tittered and a sight blush stained her cheek. "I should hope not indeed," she replied. "I find the idea of anyone *leaping,* as you put it, quite repulsive, even after marriage."

Rory bit down a response and changed the subject. "What good works did you perform the days I was gone?" he said with a smile. "You will appreciate I automatically assumed that you were engaged in something worthwhile."

"It's true I believe in keeping busy," she said, relieved the subject had moved onto safer ground. "I sew for the St. Winifred's orphanage. The girls do seem to get so damp and crumpled. I've been making pinafores for them."

"It's not surprising they get in that state," replied Lord Dexter. "They spend their time doing laundry and ironing for customers who pay for the service. Not that they used to see any of the money. I believe things are a little better now."

The place was another of his charities and he had made it a condition of his support that a sum be put aside for the girls against the day they were forced out into the world. He never spoke of this, and did not do so now.

"I'm astonished you are aware of it," responded his intended. "I know nothing of all that, and have no desire to know. But I'm glad to hear the young women are learning a useful occupation. They are drawn from the lowest class of society and it's not to be supposed they can amount to anything. Their mothers are mostly unwed or simply leave them at the door. They are lucky to be taken in."

"Does your Christianity not teach you *inasmuch as ye have done it unto one of the least of these my brethren*, and so on?"

"Indeed it does, and that is why I sew for the orphanage. Can you doubt it?"

"Of course not, my dear," was Lord Dexter's reply, but secretly he thought that charity without respect for the object of it was no real charity at all, and he thankfully took his leave.

Chapter Forty-Two

London 1816

It was a day or so later that Miss Warner received the missive from Edwin Price. She had been aware of his interest in her when he was her father's curate, and in her lukewarm way had expected a proposal from him. When his curacy had come to an end without a declaration and he had left for Kent, she had been conscious of a sense of disappointment. It was under these circumstances she had accepted Rory Compton. She was now assailed by doubts, increasingly aware that his idea of marital relations and her own were far different.

She had as model only her parents, between whom only the mildest degree of affection was evident. Indeed, her mother stood in such awe of her fine husband that she scarcely expected more than the tepid regard he bestowed on her. He was a man who loved no one more than himself. His wife both loved and admired him, but with the sort of love and admiration one might feel for a work of art, rather than a real man. The coupling that had produced Philippa had been one of the rare examples of physical intimacy that had graced their marriage. She expected no more and he, thinking himself above the common man, had no more to give.

The letter from Edwin was a model of the epistolary art that seeks to hide what it wishes to reveal:

The Parsonage, Sheld, Kent

My dear Miss Warner,

You are no doubt surprised to hear from me, though I believe our relationship such that you will not be altogether astonished. I think I am right that the friendship existing between us at the time of my departure was of an uncommon nature.

You may know that I have been lucky enough to receive a living from The Earl of Sheld, who, amongst his other properties, has a fine estate near Sevenoaks in Kent. It is there I have the honor to serve the Countess and the Dowager Countess, the Earl himself being often absent, due to press of business.

The busy town of Sevenoaks being the natural center of a vibrant local life, it was there I happened to be dining the other day when I observed the gentleman whom I believe to be the lucky aspirant to your hand. The lady with whom Lord Dexter was seated appeared delighted with him, as who would not? Such a gentleman in both figure and address!

The relationship between them was, I gathered from their ease of intercourse, of long acquaintance. I am not happy enough to know the lady in question, though I believe I heard Lord Dexter call her Héloise. I have no doubt a lady of such beauty and charm must be well known to you who are so much better

*acquainted than I with fashionable London. I
happened to be in the yard after lunch, and saw
them leave together in the direction of London. No
doubt Lord Dexter will have conveyed that lady's
best wishes and congratulations to you.*

*I am sure, dear Miss Warner, that no gentleman
having the felicity to call you his betrothed needs
any good wishes from me. I send them only to you,
therefore, and assure you now, and always, of my
most devoted admiration. Please know that I
consider the moments I was permitted to spend in
your company when working with your esteemed
father the happiest of my life.*

Yours in the love of Our Lord and Savior,
Edwin Price

Philippa raised her eyes from this letter with a sigh. Here was the proper expression of a gentleman! Here was the sweet sensibility, the charming tenderness, the exalted generosity, and the refinement of thought Fordyce had described! It was clear the worthy man loved her but was too delicate to express it directly. And he was ready to give the purest of motives to what was clearly an assignation of the vilest sort.

And as for Dexter! So, he had been on the road to London with that... that *woman*. For, of course, she was perfectly well aware of what Héloise was, even though she would never pronounce the word, even to herself. He had claimed to be in Hastings *with a friend*. It was now all too clear who that friend was. And yet he had vowed to give up all that sort of thing. How dare he? Had he so little care for her reputation that he allowed himself to be seen... well, in her imagination he might as well as been in the

251

arms of the woman. It was atrocious! It was unimaginable! It was the worst of all insults! Philippa lashed herself into a fury.

A martial light in her eye that would have done justice to Joan of Arc or Boadicea as they prepared to face the foe, she called to her plain-faced duenna (for even in her fury she did not forget the proprieties), jammed her hat upon her head, put on her pelisse as those warriors would have donned a breastplate, and sallied forth. With her hand before her like a staff, she hailed a hackney and climbed in, her handmaiden humbly behind her.

"Dexter House, Hans Square," she directed.

In a very few minutes she was at her destination. She strode purposefully up the steps and rapped on the door with such ferocity that Wolfe, the butler, sprang forth from his *loge* like a startled hare and opened and re-closed it almost before the duenna had finished paying the hackney driver and mounted the front steps. She scuttled through the narrowing space and stood in the hall.

"Take me to Lord Dexter. I wish to speak to him!" she looked and sounded like a fury.

"Yes, Miss, but may I take your your…," stammered the poor man.

"No! I do not intend to spend a moment more in this house of infamy than absolutely necessary. Lead me to him at once!"

Rory was just pouring himself a second glass of sherry when the drawing room door was abruptly opened and his fiancée stormed in ahead of the butler, whose words of presentation were frozen on his lips. He stood and, replacing the bottle on the table, came towards her.

"Philippa! What a pleasa…."

He got no further.

"Do not call me that!" she snapped. "I have not given you leave to use my Christian name, nor shall I ever do so! I have no desire to join the ranks of those you address in that way, most recently, I am told, Héloise Ramsay. I have learned she was the "friend" you visited in Hastings. It is useless to deny it. Did you think I should remain in ignorance? But be sure your sins shall find you out!"

Rory was astonished. "But my dear, I assure you…."

"I am glad to say I am not now, nor shall ever be, your *dear.*"

So saying, she wrenched the engagement ring he had given her from her finger and threw it across the room in his direction.

"There, take this back. The jewels of Satan! Just as he tempted Our Lord, you thought to win me by your riches while contaminating me with your tongue. I see now how you sought to persuade me from the path of righteousness by your insinuating arguments! And look at you, sitting here drinking spirituous liquors, of course! What else should I expect from a man of such low morals and evil habits. You disgust me."

She stalked to the door, where the butler and her duenna were both transfixed, open-mouthed. There, she turned and said, "I shall be sending a note to *The Gazette* that our engagement is at an end. There is no more to be said."

She went swiftly to the front door, too swiftly for Wolfe who arrived after she had opened it, and was in time only to bow to the duenna as she hurried out behind her mistress, distressed but not surprised. She liked Lord Dexter very much and had always thought him much too good for Miss Warner.

Back in the drawing room, Rory returned slowly to his chair by the fire and brought the sherry wonderingly to his lips. But before it got there, he noticed something glinting on the carpet. He stooped down and picked it up. It was the engagement ring. A broad smile split his face, and when the butler came back, he found his lordship leaning back in his chair, roaring with laughter.

Chapter Forty-Three

London 1816

Philippa was as good as her word. Not more than twenty-four hours after her stormy interview with Lord Dexter, the announcement ending their engagement appeared in the newspapers. Héloise saw it and in spite of herself, her heart leaped. She had not seen him since their return from Hastings. She had stopped going out and was spending her time winding up her affairs in London. She thought of Rory often, but made no attempt to see him.

A few days later she received a letter in an unknown hand. It proved to be from Lord Dexter's man of business.

> *Dear Mrs. Ramsay,*
> *I write on behalf of his lordship Rory Compton, Lord Dexter. He has instructed me to send you the enclosed draft on his bank for the purposes he laid before you during a recent sojourn in Hastings.*
> *You will remember that at that time his lordship undertook to pay for the education of your son Emile at Eton and, should he prove able enough, which his lordship fully expects, at Oxford. Lest you should*

consider this unusual, let me assure you that this is only one of the many charitable investments Lord Dexter makes in the field of education.

The balance of the draft is intended for the purchase of a suitable house for your mother and her friends Agnès and Joseph. This is in grateful thanks for the careful nursing and nourishing cuisine they provided during his recent illness, and without which would he most certainly have perished.

His lordship wishes you to understand that this payment in no way renders you indebted to him. He regards the second part as re-payment for services and the first as an investment in the future of an English gentleman.

Yours sincerely,

Theodore Monkton, Esquire

For and on behalf of Rory Compton, Lord Dexter.

The draft was for the sum of twenty thousand pounds. Héloise stared at it in wonderment. It represented exactly the balance of the sum she had hoped to make by spending another year as a courtesan in the capital. How generous he was! But could she possibly accept such a sum? Then she reflected that the letter referred only to a charitable donation and payment for services. There was nothing personal in it. He had not written himself, nor made any attempt to see her. It would allow her to leave this life she hated and carry through the plans she had made for her son and her family. She decided to accept it and sat down to write a letter of thanks, not to Rory himself, but to his man of business. She would be professional, too.

Dear Mr. Monkton,

Please convey to Lord Dexter the profoundest gratitude of my son and my mother for his generosity in providing for the education of the one and the suitable housing of the other.

He may rest assured that my son Emile will fulfill to his utmost the confidence that his lordship places in him, and that my mother will remember his name daily in her prayers.

It remains only for me to add my own sincerest thanks for his goodness towards us. He has done for them what I could not.

Yours sincerely,

Héloïse Rambuteau

She spent the rest of the week making the final arrangements for the disposal of her furniture and effects, made a generous payment to the Simpkins and returned to Hastings.

Philippa Warner wrote back to Edwin Price thanking him for the information he had so kindly given her. Her letter was, of course, couched with delicacy, but, unlike his, it practiced no dissimulation. Her meaning was very clear. After the usual greetings, she wrote:

Combined with the misgivings I was already experiencing about the delicacy of his lordship's mind, his clandestine liaison with the woman you described convinced me to end our betrothal. I will not say what she is; I believe I can leave you to guess, if you have not guessed already.

I feel as if a load has been removed from my shoulders, and I find myself returning to the memories of a golden girlhood in which, may I say it, you appear as both confidant and dear friend.

I am delighted to hear of your preferment. The situation sounds delightful. I am sure that with the constant company of such refined persons as the Countess and the Dowager, the distance from the Capital cannot be regarded as a disadvantage. To the contrary, as my own experience has so recently made clear, it must be a delight to be so far from the low morals and disgusting behavior one so frequently encounters here. I would find it a veritable paradise.

It is not to be supposed that the Reverend Price did not take the hint. He invited her to visit. She went, with her plain-faced duenna, of course. She admired, he peacocked. The announcement of their betrothal was made two months later.

Her parents were disappointed, he because he fancied being the father of a peeress, she because she far preferred Lord Dexter to the vain young curate she had known so well. But it was, in fact, a perfect match. Their intercourse was an exact representation of the feelings described by Fordyce, so admired by them both. If it lacked passion, neither of them noticed.

Lord Dexter resumed his life in London, his sense of relief that his betrothal was at an end was even greater than Philippa's. He wondered now why he had entered into it in the first place. He must have been mad. He was never to know who had spilled the beans, so to speak, about Hastings, but he would certainly have shaken that person warmly by the hand if they had ever met.

But as the days turned into weeks and the weeks turned into a month, then two, he missed Héloise not less, but more every day. Sir Harry Brothers, the would-be lover she had put off before leaving for Hastings, never stopped talking about her and was loud in his chagrin.

"Told me she had a family emergency and was leaving town, probably forever," he said during a game of cards one day in the club. "Damned shame. Place seems empty without her."

Rory agreed. He wasn't surprised Héloise had disappeared from the London scene, but tried to tell himself it was just as well she had. He threw himself back into a life of such gaiety and dissipation that even had it not been true of him before, Miss Warner's description of him was certainly warranted now. He gambled ferociously, drank too much, astonished even his friends with his outrageous behavior and scorched his way through a number of women. But he couldn't forget Héloise.

It was after three months of this, that his mother summoned him.

"Rory, dear," she said, "you know I don't usually interfere with your life. Indeed, that's why I moved out of Dexter House, but now I'm forced to say something. What on earth is the matter with you? We had a quiet little chat about your future and you ran off and got engaged to that dreadful girl. I knew she didn't suit you, and of course she didn't. I don't know how you got rid of her, and I should be glad you did, except that your carryings-on over the past couple of months have been appalling! Everywhere I go someone is recounting the latest: apparently the day before yesterday you wagered you could drink five bottles of champagne at Lady Evelynne's, and stood on the dining table to do so. Having won the wager, you fell backwards and if the footmen hadn't caught you, you would certainly have struck your head on that Boule cabinet of hers and probably killed yourself, not to mention the damage to the cabinet."

"Pity I didn't crash into the damned thing," answered her son sullenly. "I've always hated it."

"No, you haven't," said his Mama calmly, "what you hate at the moment is yourself. Why?"

Rory was going to toss off some silly answer, but suddenly he knew he had to tell the truth, or he'd go mad.

"Oh, Mama!" He collapsed into a chair and put his head in his hands. "It's Héloise. I just can't get her out of my mind. I miss her. I want her. I don't think I can live without her."

"Do you mean Mrs. Ramsay?" asked his mother in astonishment. "I didn't think you knew her above a slight acquaintance. I never heard you were one of her lovers."

"I wasn't. I wanted to be, but she kept refusing. But then she had a problem and asked me for help."

And the whole story came out. The illegitimate son, the inn in Hastings, the challenge to Protheroe, his collapse, the confession he'd overhead Héloise make to her mother, everything.

His mother took it all in and looked at him calmly. "But why on earth don't you ask her to marry you?"

He stared at her. "But what about the family honor? How can I marry a woman… like that?"

"You mean a woman who made a mistake when she was fifteen, who did the only thing she could do to provide for her family? A woman who, from what I can tell, loves you as much as you love her? I think the family honor can bear it."

Lord Dexter looked at his mother. "You can't mean it! Think of the scandal! People will say I've run mad. We'll be a laughing stock."

"If it means you'll settle down and live a sober family life instead of threatening our friends' furniture and making a fool of yourself, I think a few months of scandal will be worth it. As for being a laughing stock, if marrying a courtesan will make you happy, I will willingly bear it, and more. I perfectly understand Mrs. Ramsay doing what she did for the sake of her son. I would have done it, too, my love. You are more precious to me than any so-called honor."

Rory bolted up from his chair, pulled his mother to her feet, and enveloped her in a crushing embrace. He kissed her resoundingly on the cheek and said, "Thank you, Mama, I have to go now."

"Go? Where to?"

"Hastings," he replied.

Chapter Forty-Four

Hastings 1816

Héloise was helping Agnès hang out the washing when Emile came running into the back garden of the *Traveller's Rest.*

"Maman!" he cried, "He's here!"

"Who's here, chéri?" she replied calmly, though her heart gave a great leap and she dropped the clothes pegs she was holding.

"The monsieur from the duel who was sick and said I was his son, but I don't think I am, am I?"

He looked up at her with her own wide grey eyes.

"No, chéri, but he is our good friend."

She had no time to say more, for the object of their discussion came striding through the grass and, without stopping to say a word, threw his curly-brimmed beaver hat to the ground, caught her up in his arms and kissed her.

Emile looked at them with astonishment. His maman had said this man was not his father, but here he was kissing her and she was letting him! He was glad his friends weren't there to see it.

"Don't you dare say *No* to me one more time, Héloïse Rambuteau," said Lord Dexter, when he finally let her go. "Or I shan't be responsible for my actions."

Agnès, who although she still had difficulty in speaking English, could understand it pretty well by now, muttered, "I can't believe you said *No* to him at all, but if you're going to do it again, please go somewhere else to do it. These sheets won't dry themselves and you're in my way."

She had spoken in French, but Lord Dexter, who understood her perfectly well said, "You're not going to say it again, so let's help Agnès with the washing and all go inside to toast our engagement."

So saying, he took hold of a handful of damp linen and, picking up the clothes pegs Héloïse had dropped, began to pin it inexpertly to the washing line.

Emile, who had been watching all this time, laughed in delight as the man who he liked a great deal and who he now vaguely understood wanted to become his father, pinned great handfuls of linen haphazardly to the line.

"But you can't mean...," began Héloïse and then stopped and laughed with her son. "You can't mean to marry me and you can't hang a sheet like that! It will crease dreadfully and the wind can't get in to dry it! Look! This is how you do it."

And she showed him how to peg two corners first, well stretched out, then peg the corners of the other end just inside the others so that the linen was slightly pouched on the windward side.

"Now the wind can puff it out like a sail. You'll see!"

"I do see. I never imagined science was involved in hanging out the washing."

"No, like most things women do expertly, it's just taken for granted." She stopped and thought for a moment, then said seriously, "But, truly, Lord Dexter, you cannot marry me. You know you cannot!"

"I not only can, my mother says I must, to protect our friends' furniture." He smiled at her incomprehension. "And to stop me from going mad. Héloise, I can't live without you. That's all there is to it. I've loved you from the first moment I saw you. It drove me to distraction seeing you with those other men. And my name is Rory. Rory Compton."

To the delight of Agnès, and the unbridled amusement of Emile, Lord Dexter went down on one knee, there in the grass, and said, "Héloise Rambuteau, will you do me the immense honor of becoming my wife? I even promise to learn how to hang out the washing and do it every day, if you say yes."

Héloise smiled at him. "In that case, Rory Compton, yes I will marry you." She took his hand, and pulled him to his feet. "But you'd best leave the washing to the experts. And Emile, stop laughing and come and make your bow to Lord Dexter."

"Is he going to be my father?"

"Yes, he is. And he's really a very important man, so you'd better not make fun of him."

But since the very important man was amusing himself by seeing if he could get one of the clothes pegs to stay on his nose, Emile simply went off in another peal of laughter.

Then they finished pegging out the wash and all went inside to celebrate.

Epilogue

Three months later, Rory Compton, Lord Dexter, and Héloise Rambuteau were married in St. George's Chapel. Héloise had suggested a quiet wedding in her own parish, but Rory was having none of it.

"What? And let people think I'm ashamed of marrying you in the face of all the *ton?* Certainly not! I shall marry you with as much pomp and ceremony as if you were the daughter of the King of England."

And on the day, along with the cream of London society, the Prince Regent himself came down the aisle—late, of course, just before the bride was set to appear. He had always liked Dexter, he said, damned fine fellow, up for any wager you care to name. And the bride was a good-looking filly. He wished he'd got to her first. In the front pews on the other side of the aisle from the Prince, sat the bride's mother, next to her faithful friend, Agnès Thomas. An immensely proud Joseph Thomas walked Héloise down the aisle, unable to believe that the little girl he'd made applewood clothes hooks for was marrying into the British peerage. As his friend Bernard would have said, it was the Revolution in action.

Emile went to Eton where he distinguished himself not so much by his scholarship but by his willingness to try anything, and his mastery at conkers. As he got older and would-be bullies tried to torment him about his mother's earlier profession, he would always say, *better to begin a whore and end up a lady than the reverse,* as he heard was the case in their own family. In this way he was often involved in fisticuffs, but since Rory taught him the fine art of pugilism, he was rarely challenged twice.

Claire split her time between the Dexter homes and *The Traveller's Rest* where Agnès and Joseph stayed. It was their home, they said. Upon their retirement, Lord and Lady Dexter bought them a fine house opposite the sea in the center of Hastings.

They never went back to France. England had been good to them, said Agnès. *Verray will, zank yew.*

The End

A Note from the Author

If you enjoyed this novel, please leave a review! Go to the Amazon page and scroll down past all the other books Amazon wants you to buy(!) till you get to the review click. Thank you so much! This is the link:

For a free short story and to listen to the author read the first chapter of all her novels, please go to the website:

https://romancenovelsbyglrobinson.com

Regency Novels by GL Robinson

Please go to my Amazon Author Pages for more information:

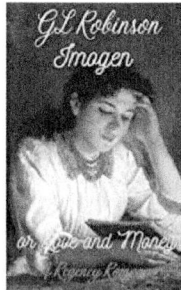

Imogen or Love and Money Lovely young widow Imogen is pursued by Lord Ivo, a well-known rake. She angrily rejects him and concentrates on continuing her late husband's business enterprises. But will she find that money is more important than love?

Cecilia or Too Tall to Love Orphaned Cecilia, too tall and too outspoken for acceptance by the *ton,* is determined to open a school for girls in London's East End slums, but is lacking funds. When Lord Tommy Allenby offers her a way out, will she get more than she bargained for?

Rosemary or Too Clever to Love Governess Rosemary is forced to move with her pupil, the romantically-minded Marianne, to live with the girl's guardian, a strict gentleman with old fashioned ideas about young women should behave. Can she save the one from her own folly and persuade the other that she isn't just a not-so-pretty face?

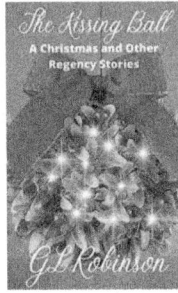

The Kissing Ball A collection of Regency short stories, not just for Christmas. All sorts of seasons and reasons!

The Earl and The Mud-Covered Maiden *The House of Hale Book One*. When a handsome stranger covers her in mud driving too fast and then lies about his name, little does Sophy know her world is about to change forever.

The Earl and His Lady *The House of Hale Book Two.* Sophy and Lysander are married, but she is unused to London society and he's very proud of his family name. It's a rocky beginning for both of them.

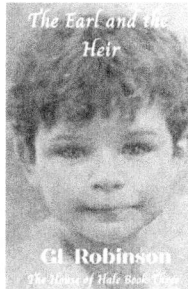

The Earl and The Heir *The House of Hale Book Three.* The Hale family has a new heir, in the shape of Sylvester, a handful of a little boy with a lively curiosity. His mother is curious too, about her husband's past. They both get themselves in a lot of trouble.

The Lord and the Red-Headed Hornet Orphaned Amelia talks her way into a man's job as secretary to a member of the aristocracy. She's looking for a post in the Diplomatic Service for her twin brother. But he wants to join the army. And her boss goes missing on the day he is supposed to show up for a wager. Can feisty Amelia save them both?

The Lord and the Cat's Meow A love tangle between a Lord, a retired Colonel, a lovely debutante, and a fierce animal rights activist. But Horace the cat knows what he wants. He sorts it out.

The Lord and the Bluestocking The Marquess of Hastings is good-looking and rich but is a little odd. Nowadays he would probably be diagnosed as having Asperger's syndrome. To find a wife he scandalizes the *ton* by advertising in the newspaper. Elisabeth Maxwell is having no luck finding a publisher for her children's book and is willing to marry him to escape an overbearing stepfather. This gently amusing story introduces us to an unusual but endearing Regency couple. The question is: can they possibly co-exist, let alone find happiness?

About The Author

GL Robinson is a retired French professor who took to writing Regency Romances in 2018. She dedicates all her books to her sister, who died unexpectedly that year and who, like her, had a lifelong love of the genre. She remembers the two of them reading Georgette Heyer after lights out under the covers in their convent boarding school and giggling together in delicious complicity.

Brought up in the south of England, she has spent the last forty years in upstate New York with her American husband. She likes gardening, talking with her grandchildren and sitting by the fire. She still reads Georgette Heyer.

Keep reading for a preview of GL Robinson's next Regency Romance, available in the Fall!

Beatrix meets the Baron and his dog Juno

Meanwhile, Lukas had arrived at the family townhouse in London. He jumped down from the curricle with Juno at his heels, throwing the reins to one of the boys who loitered on the linkway to earn a few pence by performing just that service.

He mounted the front steps and hammered on the knocker.

"Baron, sir!" exclaimed the elderly servant who opened the door. He was one of those who had come with them from Germany.

"Fritz! Good to see you," said Lukas, shaking the hand of the old retainer. "Is my mother in the drawing room?"

"No, sir. She is from home. She left yesterday. With her maid."

"But didn't she receive my note that I was returning to London?"

"I think not, Baron. A letter arrived just a few minutes ago written in your hand addressed to the Baroness. Naturally, I did not open it. It's there on the hall table."

Lukas picked up the letter and saw the problem. In his haste he had written the direction very poorly and it had obviously been delivered at first to the wrong address.

"Where has she gone?"

"I'm afraid I cannot say, sir."

"Did she say when she would be back?"

"No sir, but her maid had some bags. I gathered they would be gone some while."

"Did my sister accompany her?"

"No, Baron. Fraülein Margarethe left today not long ago. She was picked up by a young man in a smart carriage. She had two bandboxes with her. She was in something of a hurry. I don't know where she was going."

"What young man?"

"I'm afraid I cannot say, sir."

"Was her maid with her?"

"No, sir."

The information might have been more complete had the regular butler been there. But the Baroness had given him and most of the other servants the day off, and the old majordomo from Mecklenburg-Schwerin was less proficient in English than he liked to admit. He misunderstood most of what he was told. Lukas spoke to him in German, of course.

"What in heaven's name is going on here?" Lukas was more enraged by the minute. Juno heard the anger in his voice and growled. Lukas put his hand on the dog's head. "My mother is from home, heaven knows where, and my sister has gone off with a young man and two bandboxes but no maid. Does that sound like usual behavior to you?"

"No, sir. Back at home it would be most unusual. But here in London, sir, I have remarked that the young people seem to, er, intermingle much more. Customs are much freer, it seems. It is the same with dogs," he added, looking at Juno with dislike. "At home we do not keep such dogs in the house."

"Perhaps not, but this is England, and people have a different relationship with their animals. But I did not believe the behavior of young ladies to be so very different. Find her maid and ask where she has gone and with whom."

"Her maid isn't here, sir. Most of the servants have been given the day off. The Baroness knows she can rely on me."

Lukas was beginning to doubt this could be true. "Do you know the names of any of my sister's friends? Think, man! Someone must know where she is!"

"She is often in the company of a Lady Beatrix, sir. A most charming young lady, if I may say."

Lukas remembered the name from Margarethe's letter.

"Yes, I understand she is given to the freedom of conduct you referred to just now. If anyone knows the reason for this extraordinary behavior it will be she. Find me someone who can give me the direction of Lady Beatrix Shelby."

A few minutes later, furnished with Trixie's address by one of the footmen who had carried frequent notes between the two houses, Lukas was driving his tired horses through the streets of London, with Juno again at his feet, her nose on his boots.

By the time Lukas arrived at Uncle Leonard's town house in Grosvenor Square, the débacle over Chauncey's phaeton was over. Lady Shelby had been carried up to her room by two of the unfortunate footmen who were beginning to wonder whether the excellent wages their employer paid them were worth the backbreaking exercise imposed on them. She was moaning gently on her bed as her abigail wafted burned feathers under her nose.

Trixie and Mariah were in the salon. Having fully thrashed out the question as to whether Chauncey was wise or foolish to ignore his Mama, and whether he would indeed break his neck with his ridiculous new vehicle, they were now engaged in a lively discussion of the appearance of various female members of the ton at the last ball. Mariah had been particularly struck by one dashing lady, not quite in her first youth, appearing in scarlet silk with pink roses that she would have liked for herself. "Tasteless" was Trixie's estimation, a position she held to in spite of Mariah's hot denials.

They were therefore astonished when the butler opened the door and, somewhat flustered, announced, "The Baron von Schwerin.". Normally a placid man with an air of authority, he had not been able to withstand the tall, commanding figure with a growling dog at his side, demanding to see the Lady Beatrix at once.

The two ladies stared at their visitor in wonder. Lukas von Schwerin was extremely good-looking in a stern, square-jawed way. Like his sister, he was very fair but whereas her eyes were of a pale blue, his were piercingly so. He looked exactly like the hero of a Romance.

He was dressed with perfect propriety and even style, but not quite in the London mode. He was in his riding boots, not normally acceptable in a drawing room, with a long dark green cloak with a single cape, fastened at the top and thrown back over his broad shoulders to reveal a well-cut wool riding coat, sober waistcoat, and britches. The points of his shirt collar were conservative, as was his neckcloth. And a large yellow dog was at his side. It was clearly a gun dog, and not the sort of animal generally seen in the salons of Mayfair.

It is not too much to say he took their breath away. For Mariah, he seemed to have walked right out of one of her novels.

He was tall, strong and handsome. With his faithful hound, he was ready to rescue any maiden from distress, no matter how hideous. Trixie's reaction was more primal. She felt a lurch in her stomach she had never experienced before. She felt herself flushing; she caught her breath. For the first time in her life it was not her head that reacted to a man, but her whole being.

****

283

Printed in Great Britain
by Amazon